# THIS STORIED LAND

lou mandler

www.pronghornpress.org

*In memory of my parents—*

*who created a loving
and safe environment
in a harsh world.*

# Acknowledgments

This book appears after a very long journey on which a patchwork of forums and the generosity of readers and other writers contributed to its completion.

At the beginning, a Klingenstein Fellowship from Teachers' College of Columbia University brought me to the classrooms of Frank McShane and Claudia Bushman where I first began to commemorate my childhood on Montana's Hi-Line. June Bale Wassel's writing circle at Hartford College for Women took me another mile. I owe more than I can express to Anne Batterson and her wise and gracious leadership of our writers' group. The entire group—Louise Feldman, Carolyn Soutter, Pam Kelly, and Sherry Horton— kept me going with their comments and encouragement. Sherry gave a particularly helpful reading of one of the last drafts. Sara Blackburn's skilled eye and active pencil breathed life into the first draft.

Along the way, a few precious summer weeks at Bard College's Writing Retreat for Teachers gave me time and the encouragement of Myra McLarey. Patricia Hampel and Carol Houck Smith offered crucial guidance at the Bread Loaf Writers' Conference. My Headmaster and friend, Tom Sheehy, let me play hooky for several valuable weeks of focus. My friend Lue Ponich invited me to The High Plains BookFest in Billings where I met my publisher, Annette Chaudet, who has given unstintingly of her time and advice.

I thank all my siblings for sharing their memories, for correcting details, for maintaining our sense of family. My older brother, whose brain is crammed with information, provided invaluable advice both on structuring the book and on facts about farming and wildlife. I am grateful to those siblings who have shown enthusiasm for this book, and I am grateful to those siblings who, despite their unease over putting our family in the public eye, have exhibited a calm forbearance. My aunt and uncle, my mother's sister and brother, were also helpful and supportive.

And then there's JP, my husband, friend, and frankest critic, who did his best to keep my sentences correct and my emotional tone unsentimental. He knows the rest.

*The weaver-god, he weaves; and by that weaving is he deafened, that he hears no mortal voice; and by that humming, we, too, who look on the loom are deafened; and only when we escape it shall we hear the thousand voices that speak through it.*

—Herman Melville, *Moby Dick*

# Contents

## Part Three: Harvest

lou mandler

# Prologue

# The Hood Wearer

The sharp smell of drying leaves stirred memories of other, colder fall days two thousand miles to the west. The lush surroundings of the small Connecticut boarding school where I work don't often bring me back to my childhood on the Montana prairie, but sometimes a whiff of an earth scented March breeze, the squeak of snow underfoot, or a banner of rose light in the western sky evokes my other, earlier world. And today the smell of drying vegetation.

Perhaps the reminder came more easily because of yesterday's scene still flickering in my sight brain. It was one of those pictures that you stumble upon and suddenly the past comes tumbling into your mind. I had been walking down the street with my daughter, and we came upon a young man welding. Just that. But the leaping arcs of light and the crouching figure topped in a black hood immediately put me in my father's farm shop and its mingled smells of the dirt floor, grease, oil, and fire. I saw again the concentration of my father, bending over his forge as he performed the miracle of making metal bend, or crouching beside his welder as he fused metal pieces to repair his machinery.

I was seven when my father bought a new red welder. He wore a black hood with an isinglass rectangle over the eyes when he welded, and when he lowered the hood to cover his face, he sent us away. My mother told us it was dangerous to be near the welder, and my sister Vivien said we would go blind if we looked at the sparks without the isinglass protection he had in his hood. So the miracles the welder saw were not miracles we could observe. Only he could see the metal transforming. I was envious of this vision we couldn't share, and very curious about it. We were intrigued by the way our father disappeared under his black hood. But his disappearance wasn't so different from the times he would stand and gaze at the horizon, and none of us knew what our tall and gentle father was thinking.

Only our mother seemed to understand a little of the pain and mystery under the hood and behind the distant gaze. As she kept us from the sparks of welding for our safety, so she seemed to want to protect the welder from injury. Our mother's best instrument in her guardian role were her words and stories.

So we grew, zigzagging between mystery and stories.

# This Storied Land

lou mandler

Part One

# The Crucible

lou mandler

# One

# The View Through the Window

"You know, people don't like to talk about family troubles in those books," my mother says. "But if you happen to know about them, well, it makes a difference."

My mother and I sit together at the wooden table in my parents' Montana farm kitchen. Between us lies one of "those books," a fat history of the county. Stories of individual farm families, penned by a family member, fill the pages. I had left my husband and family behind in Connecticut to come "home" for my annual summer visit. My mother is near eighty, and this summer I know more than ever that

# lou mandler

I will not always be able to sit at this table of memories, see my mother sitting at her place, listen to her stories, and read the meaning of her silences.

She sits gazing out the big bay window at the ripening wheat fields to the south. Her winter's illness has thinned her face and taken some of the softness from her small frame, but a suggestion remains of the full hips and arms of the mother who raised us. Her body has borne and nursed nine children, seven daughters and two sons. The table where we now sit has supported our food and elbows; witnessed our arguments, jokes, silences, and stories for nearly fifty years. Throughout the seasons of my childhood, my mother and father sat at either end, anchoring the table and our lives.

My mother lived all her life within a four-mile radius of this section of Montana's hilly plains. The eastern edge of the state's Hi-Line, the strip of plains tucked just beneath the Canadian border, lies so far from the westward route of the Oregon Trail and the path taken to the California gold mines that the first white settlers did not come here until the 1880s. These seekers came to work on the ranches the cattle companies had started fifty miles to the south, along the Missouri River. With the completion of the Great Northern railroad and its competitor, the Soo Line, around 1910, this remote country began filling with homesteaders, dirt farmers.

By 1920, ten thousand people lived in our county. They came mostly from the east, from Minnesota and North Dakota, or from Norway, Sweden, Denmark, and Germany. They came hoping to earn a good living from the soil that produced such plentiful prairie grass. Fifty years later, in 1970, after the drought of the 1930s, scores of hailstorms, dozens of grasshopper plagues, and years of industrialization, ten thousand had dwindled to six thousand. By 1995, just over four thousand people lived in the county's eighteen hundred square miles. All that remains of Hunter, the little town two miles north of us, once home to hundreds, is a gray, once white, steepled church and the tiny square jail.

Most of the farmers who came to wrest a living out of the sulky but grandiloquent land of northern Montana were Scandinavians—Swedes like my mother's family; Norwegians; and Danes with names like Johnson, Larson, Sorenson, Brensdahl, Lidahl, Lagerquist, Knutson, Madsen— but an enclave of Russians lived in a section of land marked by coulees, where my mother grew up. Mysteriously, it was called Dutch Coulee. And the huge Morgan clan certainly wasn't Scandinavian. Joe Morgan, one of seven sons, lived two miles west of Dutch Coulee. Like the Old Testament Joseph, Joe and his family became "a multitude of people." The Morgans were everywhere when I was growing up, and Joe himself begat twelve children. He would turn out to be an important person in our own family story.

By the time my mother was born, the native Assinboine Indians had been pushed onto reservations to the south and west. But even in my time, we had the sense that the Indians had left just the other day. Our farm had been Chippewa land until 1922 when Jens Ibsen, who later sold it to my father, bought it.

As a child walking in our pastures, I could feel the presence of the people who had arranged the stones on top of Eagle Hill, who had shaped the grinding stone my father discovered one day in his field. The buffalo round, a huge rock in one of our wheat fields, sunken some fifteen feet into the earth, reminded us of the buffalo who had rubbed their hairy sides against it for centuries. The circle of the buffalo round and the occasional ring of rock in the pastures suggested a long-ago pattern for living. But the buffalo and the native Indians and their stories were long gone, and we could only guess at the purpose of the stone designs, mostly rough circular patterns, beside the sloughs and on the tops of hills.

When I was growing up in the 1950s and in my mother's childhood in the 1920s and 30s, the local Indians had come from elsewhere—the neighboring state of North Dakota, just north of us in Canada, or other counties south and west. What we children knew of the Indians, or of any of our neighbors, we knew because talking came naturally to our mother. Mama gave the land of our childhood a rich history through her stories of those who had lived here.

Mama didn't think there were any bad Indians. She told us that when she was a child, her family's closest neighbors were Henry Larsson and his wife Maria, a Metis woman from North Dakota. My mother played with their daughter Annie and with the LeBruns, relatives of Maria Larsson, who also lived close by. Because of these Indian playmates, throughout her life Mama was a stalwart supporter of anything Indian. Maria Larsson was one of the Indian women Mama had in mind when she commented once, "The thing about the Indians was they were better than the white people they married."

The dry-land farm my father bought from Jens Ibsen was just over five hundred acres. By 1965, our farm had more than doubled in size with the addition of two more parcels of land. The wheat in the field strips to the south and the Aberdeen Angus cattle in the pastures to the north provided our family's livelihood. Mama and Daddy had named their

# This Storied Land

farm Eagle Hill, after the hill in the north pasture from which miles of prairie and cropland were visible in every direction. Eagle Hill reared to the sky in the section we called "Mama's land" because she had insisted that Daddy buy the 320 acres at a time he felt he couldn't afford it. We often walked to the top of Eagle Hill to see the world.

My parents grew up on the prairie in the '20s and '30s during a time when they and their parents struggled mightily to survive. Mama and Daddy had learned well the lessons the land taught during the '30s. My mother's stories, my father's actions, their watchfulness, gave me my first impressions of the land. The way my father watched the skies and walked through his wheat field, feeling the heads of the wheat. The way they listened to the radio only for the weather report and the grain and cattle prices. The way their faces showed satisfaction and well being when the abstemious skies finally let the rains fall. The land seemed a living character in our lives. My parents spent their years listening and watching for messages from the land, working out compromises with the land, making adjustments, deals.

On my own, I knew from the beginning that the land was alive because it spoke in many voices. The frogs in the slough, the crickets in the grass, the birds—the meadowlarks, the phalaropes, the blackbirds, the owls at night, the bitterns, the migrating ducks—all sounded different notes and melodies. The wind, too, spoke in many sounds and speeds. It swept in, evoking questions about where it had been, what it had seen. In the rare times when the wind was quiet, the silence of the land was powerful too. It hinted of lives lived here in times past. Of the majesty of the earth, the mystery of life, of death, of things I didn't know.

The vast space magnified the sound of man's work. When we walked through the pasture, we could hear from yards away the keening of the electric poles that marched over the plains. I remember lying in bed in a night of absolute quiet, a night full of held-breath expectation. Then two miles away the train going through Hunter hooted long and gradually faded away. Dark quiet again. Then, barely perceptible, the hum of a car coming up the gravel road from the highway. The muted throb gradually expanding, growing, becoming a roar through which the clank and click of the gravel on the metal of the car and the swish of the tires still sounded as the car purred past. Then the reverse. The roar dimming to a hum and shrinking, contracting until the silence of the earth reigned again and seemed in the stillness to remember the sound with an ache.

I always felt that even in its quiet times, our earth pulsed with restrained power. It was like a wild horse at rest, the eyes still wild and the heart still pounding. The earth and eternity seemed linked.

As I sit, recently arrived from Connecticut, with my mother at the table, she has lived more than seventy-five years on these dry plains. By now, I know I haven't always paid attention to my mother's stories, and I wish I had. But I also know that her stories have skirted a silence at the core of our existence. Her talk might veer close to her mother, but she usually catches herself, clamps her expressive mouth into unnatural firmness, and says something like, "Oh! Enough of that."

Today I want to listen so I can never forget. Despite the traces of age in my mother's face, her pink-hued Scandinavian complexion contrasts with her white hair and gives her a look of vitality. We have been chatting about the present; I want to lead her to the past. The link is the land. As we sit looking over the fields to the south, I ask for details about why my father's parents had left "this country," as my mother terms northern Montana. Her blue eyes narrow behind her glasses in that familiar focused gaze that means she is seeing other times. Eyes on our land, she begins her story. Her face is screwed up in concentrated, painful memory.

"Daddy's folks lost their land in the bad years." She usually refers to her husband by what we children called him.

"When they first came to Montana, in 1928, they rented the Hanson place. The next year they bought the Ole Aspelund place, but in 1937 the bank took it over. Those years were so hard for everyone. Things were bad all over the country, what with the Depression and all, and then to top it all off, the weather turned against the farmers.

"Some of those years in the '30s, there wasn't even enough moisture in the soil for the wheat seed to germinate. And if it happened to rain one year, it seemed like hail or grasshoppers would get the crops. Because all the crops everywhere in the county failed, people couldn't even sell their machinery.

"Times were really rough. My dad said about that time, 'It's harder to find twenty-five cents during this Depression than it was to find twenty-five dollars in 1928. And some people were too proud to go on the dole. So lots of people just pulled up and left. Went back to Minnesota or out to Washington or California."

She tells how Grandpa and Grandma Wiedeman moved from farm to farm until the Second World War, when they moved to Washington state, where Grandpa worked in the shipyards. This story of my grandparents' failed attempts at farming brings my mother to speak of its effect on their son, her husband.

"Daddy was always determined that he would own his own farm and not lose it like his dad did. In fact, when Jens Ibsen sold Daddy this farm, he thought sure Daddy wouldn't make a go of it, and that he, Jens, would get it back."

My mother grins and the spirit that always stands ready in her heart flashes out. "Well, I guess Daddy showed him. Why, once after he sold Daddy the land, Jens Ibsen came up to Daddy in Hunter and asked him for a penny for a penny postcard." Her triumph in my father's farming success and her pride in her marriage shines in her eyes.

But then she sobers and thinks for a time. She fingers her lip and chin in her characteristic way. The next story is unusual for its subject

"My folks lost their farm once, too. My dad couldn't pay the mortgage for a long time. Finally the man from the loan company came out to talk about the money they owed on the farm, and my dad had to sign the land over. Well, when my dad told her, she got so mad."

My mother always referred to her own mother, our grandmother, as "*she*" or "*her*." She never said "Mother" or "Mom" or the "Ma" my father called our Grandmother Wiedeman.

"Then that night my dad went outside, and I knew he was feeling bad so I followed him and he was just crying so hard. The only other time I saw him like that was when he heard his cousin in Minnesota had died. He drowned. He had been brought up with my dad because his parents were dead.

# This Storied Land

Well, that night my dad went out to the barn and cried too."

"You know," she says, "I can still see those pictures. Some things just stay in your mind where you can see them so clear."

Of all the secrets and mysteries surrounding us as we grew up, it was the one about our Olson grandparents that lived with us most. Why didn't my parents ever see or even speak to my mother's parents, our grandparents, who lived on a farm just four miles to the south and east? Throughout my childhood, we wondered. The source of this alienation seemed to be more than an argument. The secrecy my parents maintained about the Olsons suggested something shameful. We knew that whatever had happened, it had taken place some years after my parents were married, because among the photographs in my mother's desk drawer were pictures showing Mama and Daddy, in the early years of their marriage, with my mother's parents.

The photographs in the drawer and an occasional oblique reference were the only proof we had that my mother had parents. Otherwise, all was silence. Although a schoolmate of my brother's once asked him, "Do you ever see your Grandpa Olson?" I don't remember hearing anyone in the community speak to us of our grandparents. We knew no one else who had invisible relatives. Not until I was eighteen and on the verge of leaving home did I learn that my wild Swedish Grandma Olson once had my quiet, honest father arrested. While I was growing up, I suspected religion had something to do with the cause of the silence. It would be many years before I learned the facts.

I used to think that farmers believe in God because they look at the land all day, not at humanity. I don't know

now if any part of that thought is true, but I do know that people brought many religions to this country, and the different beliefs affected the relationships in our family. My mother had been brought up Lutheran, as many of the Scandinavians had been, and my father's family had once been German Lutheran. When my father was twelve, however, his parents and some of their neighbors went to Gospel meetings held by a couple of traveling preachers, and Grandpa and Grandma Wiedeman converted to the religion they were to follow for the rest of their lives. It was a religion which affected our lives as much as being a farm family did. In the years since, I have heard those outside the religion describe it as Puritanical, as Calvinist, as Quaker-like, or as a fundamentalist sect. To us, it was simply The Truth, something else that made us different.

As I watch my mother gaze at the landscape outside her window, I think of how many times we children have seen her just so—looking at the land while remembering a neighbor, a friend, a favorite animal, a dramatic event, and through her stories, we saw the land come alive. But she kept some secrets too. For years she didn't tell one of the most interesting stories, the reason she didn't speak to her mother. So it is with stories. I have stories of my own to tell, and sometimes the threads of my life and my mother's stories tangle together. In the spaces between are the silences, the stories my mother didn't tell, and my father's silent endurance. Just so are lives woven, and sometimes the silences become a story. Silence becomes picture and picture becomes story.

My mother is dead now, but I can still hear her say, "Some things just stay in your mind where you can see them so clear."

# This Storied Land

lou mandler

# Two

# Memory at Work

Outside the picture window of the living room where I sit, it is hushed, black night, nearly midnight. I must awaken in time to catch the bus to high school in the morning. I am the only one awake in the house. Only my father and I are not in bed, but he is asleep in his chair in the room where, twenty minutes ago, I finished reading a book. In the minutes since, I have been suspended between worlds; the world of my book, one fixed in eternity by the printed page, and the other world of this silent night. The night is many-ringed, my father and I in the center. Then comes the ring of sleeping brother and sisters and mother, and outside, through the dark picture window, the circle of stars, the eyes of eternal night.

In the center circle, I watch my sleeping father with new eyes. His body is slack with sleep, his head back and his mouth slightly open. His hands, loosely clasped across his abdomen, show the color of a life in the sun. Our father's hands fascinate us children. The fingers on these hands made for work taper at the ends, and the thumbs flare back from the center joint. My father's gray and white striped overalls and blue work shirt show the grease and field dirt acquired in a day's work with machinery and the soil. We are proud of our father's youthful look, his strength, his calm and wise solutions to almost any problem, but tonight as I sit alone, gazing at him, he looks vulnerable in his slumber. I realize that he will die someday. I feel the eyes of night counting minutes, years, centuries, and I feel the fleeting nature of this moment. I know my sleeping family will rise in the morning, older and closer to the eternity I feel.

The thought, feeling, image of this moment remains fixed nearly forty years later. But so memory works. It pieces together one image here, one there, and threaded together, these pieces of time preserved tell us who we are by which memories are stored, and which memories whirl into space, lost forever.

In the scenes of my very first memory, I am three. At that time, I have three older sisters and a brother and a younger infant sister. Two more sisters and the second boy, the last of us nine, are not yet born. These earliest memories are not of the crowded little house I shared as a very young child with my parents and siblings nor of the windswept farm of my childhood. Rather, the remembered scenes are of the first time when I felt lifted out of my family, when I first saw that we are alone in the world. It is a trio of pictures, burned into my brain by the strangeness of the experience.

First, it is night. I lie in a crib in a dim, unfamiliar room. This room is bigger and barer than any room in our house. The window is a pale rectangular glow in the wall. On the opposite wall, the door to a hallway stands open, showing a brightly lit but uninhabited world outside the room. I hear no one. I see no one. I cry out. Suddenly the blurred outline of a man, dressed in white, appears beside my crib, and this ghostly figure stands looking down at me. I scream.

Then it is bright day. I am in the same room, the same crib. Again I am alone. I am holding a red and white ball. I put it up to the slats in the crib to see if it will go through. Yes! I lose my grasp on the ball, and it rolls towards the door and down the hall. I watch it roll slowly, a red and white ball on a black and white speckled floor. The hall is long and empty; no one brings my ball back to me. Even the scary man is gone.

Finally, I am in the back seat of a black car. My father is driving, and my oldest sister Agnes sits, not in the front with him, but in the back with me. She unwraps a piece of gum, a rare treat, and hands it to me. She also gives me her full, comforting attention. Agnes is only six years older than I am, but she is already established as a secondary mother figure whose kindness calms me when my mother's attention is distracted by illness, housework, or childcare. Agnes is my first memory of what it is to have a sister, to share the years of childhood so thoroughly that the understanding never goes away, the bond never loosens.

Our drive ends at a doctor's office, and I lie on a hard, black table while the doctor probes the back of my left leg.

# lou mandler

I feel something wet coming out of my leg. Unlike the picture of the red ball, this memory has no color. The room and the light seem drab gray, and the doctor a shape I can't look at. This memory is feeling, feeling: the hard table, big people holding me down, poking my leg until it bleeds. Agnes gives me another piece of gum on the way home.

The three-fold series ends. Then I remember not being alone but being thoroughly wedged in a family. I see my mother, my sisters, my brother, myself gathered around the supper table. It is about four years later. We are six children at the table, three on each side. We have finished eating, and our father, weary from the day's chores, has left the kitchen for a more comfortable chair. Mama sits at her end of the table.

Lacking the power accorded the older children and the liberty allowed the youngest, I have learned to watch and listen. I sit in the middle on one side, looking out at the dark night through the uncurtained window on the other side. A bare light bulb shines from the ceiling socket over the red and green and yellow oilcloth covering. The table is uncleared, and our white enameled metal plates show the leavings of our supper. The brown juice of tonight's beef roast pools in the empty meat platter in the center.

This memory begins with my mother, prodded by a question or comment from one of my sisters, telling her own story of my early sickness. Mama's plump body is relaxed in her chair. The heads of her six children are turned to her, to the brow wrinkled in reflection, the blue eyes fixed in the familiar story-telling gaze. Just before I became seriously ill, my mother said she had a prophetic dream about an alligator biting my leg off. The voices of my brother and sisters painted other parts of the picture.

My brother Arthur, his brown hair covering his forehead, said, "You screamed on and off for two days and there wasn't anywhere to go where we couldn't hear you cry. Finally, Dr. Pronin came out."

My mother said Dr. Pronin, the Jewish doctor from town, walked into the center of our tiny living room, where I lay in the metal crib my father had made with his welder before Agnes was born. Dr. Pronin looked at my swollen, multi-colored leg and ordered me to the hospital. Each time my mother told this story, she included the firm declaration, "He saved your life, you know."

My sister Agnes said, "You wouldn't swallow your pills in the hospital so the nurses put them in ice cream to trick you."

My sister Vivien, who told stories as naturally as my mother did, described one day when my father felt he should stay and work in the field instead of driving fifteen miles to visit me in the hospital. My mother spoke to him in a way no one had heard before. "Philip, you come here," she commanded. They went into the small main room where I had lain screaming in the crib a few days before. My mother closed the door. They came out, and my father and my sister Agnes went to town to see me.

My sister Diana, who had my father's lean body and active ways, remembered helping me walk again, first on tiptoe, then as the damaged muscle healed, she encouraged me to put my heel to the floor and so stretch the muscle to its former elasticity.

Each voice around the supper table would contribute to the collective memory of my sickness. The story of my early brush with death became a many-layered tale. So my own memory and my memory of the stories of my family merged. My body recorded my sickness with a dime-shaped scar on the back of my thinner left calf. My brain recorded a mixture of my memory and the suppertime stories told and retold. What was true? What was memory embroidered?

As I grew older, I gathered facts to supplement the myth surrounding my early illness. In the winter before I turned three, first whooping cough and then the mumps struck our family. My bout with whooping cough left me weak, and when the mumps followed, my body was unusually vulnerable. An abscess, a complication of the mumps, developed in my left leg. The infection festered and spread.

Usually my mother was our doctor. Her arsenal of healing consisted of bandages, pine-scented disinfectant, and a soft hand on the forehead to detect a fever. Mama's hands had had lots of experience protecting and preserving life and health. When I was five and ripped open my thigh by running into a barbed wire fence, there was no discussion of a doctor or stitches. My mother dressed the gash that healed into a four-inch scar. When my brother sliced his thumb with a hand sickle, Mama's ministering hands filled the tin basin with hot water, clouded it with pungent-smelling disinfectant, cleaned the thumb, and closed the wound. But when I lay in my crib, hot with fever and wailing from the pain of an ugly infection, her skills were not enough. She often closed her part of the suppertime story of my illness with, "Yeeaah, Dr. Pronin said that if we had kept you home a few more hours, we would have lost you."

Mama also revealed the nature of the ghost I saw hovering over my crib that night. In our tiny hospital, patients shared rooms without regard for age or malady. The white form I saw in my night terror was my alcoholic roommate, attempting clumsy comfort.

So a moment becomes a memory. The photos in our desk drawer gave face and form to our invisible relatives. In another way, our supper table, our mother's voice, and the night through the window fixed my first memories. Such deeply felt moments or startlingly vivid pictures record indelible impressions. Decades or a lifetime later the picture or feeling comes to life, aroused by a word, a smell, a face, the cast of an evening sky, the stillness of a midnight hour. And we remember the child, the father, the supper table, the stories.

lou mandler

# Three

# My Mother's Mustang

My mother didn't look like a horsewoman. Her small-boned body was soft though I didn't think of her as fat; I remember looking at the flesh rounding her white upper arms as she reached to put a plate of steaks on the table and wondering whether I, too, would have full, round arms when I became a woman. By the time I was ten, I was taller than my mother, but not as plump. Mama's belly always held the shape of a three-month pregnancy, but when she was actually pregnant, her belly lost its softness. It was almost as if her body was not her own, but one that was consigned to proving the possibility of human survival in tough times, a tough land.

Among the old photos in the drawer of the desk in our tiny living room was an especially riveting black and white photo of my mother. It shows her at fifteen, slim, dark-haired, and smiling. Her arms are wrapped around the neck of a companion, Snider, her black horse. Written in white ink on the black page below the photo are the words, "Just Snider and me, but very good friends." Something of the girl in that photo—the lift of her head, the cast of her eye— resembled our mother, but this young horsewoman was not the mother we knew.

Although Snider lived in our pastures when I was young, my mother never rode him, never threw her arms around his neck, but we knew Snider was important. Mama didn't forget about him. When icy winter snows covered the brown prairie grasses and my father came in from pitching hay to the cattle, she would ask, "Did you see Snider?"

"Oh yaah, he's doing all right," my father would respond.

We children marveled at the mysterious pairing of this man and woman. The woman kept nothing back. The man held in nearly everything. My father was usually serious. My mother could be just plain silly. When we asked idly, "What time is it?" Mama was apt to respond, "Half past kissing time and time to kiss again." My father could keep a tune and play the harmonica. My mother had no musical talent, but as she stirred a pudding or stewed tomatoes on the stove, she sometimes launched into off-key song: "Git along little dogies . . ." She kept her silliness and her slingshot-retort ability within the family. Others didn't know that side of her. They knew only that when she heard a funny story or comment, her entire body moved with her laughter.

# This Storied Land

My mother's life with us gave her few opportunities to feed her interest in the lives of others. In the early 1950s, telephones hadn't come to our remote area, and few people visited us. Only Leonard Norman, our bachelor neighbor with the wooden leg, came regularly. He had discovered my father's patient mechanical know-how and brought his broken machinery and his tales of farmer woes to my father almost daily.

When not receiving farming counseling or mechanical help from our father, Leonard often sat in our kitchen exchanging stories with our mother. He would sit on one of the wooden kitchen chairs, pulling the loose flesh of his crepy throat, as they visited about whose cattle had gotten into which neighbor's wheat field or who had died, been born, become ill. My mother savored each conversation, bit of news, or funny story from a visitor and retold them dozens of times.

Mama liked talking about horses nearly as much as she liked telling stories about people. It seemed odd to hear her talk about horses and cattle while we watched her shell peas for dinner, fill dozens of canning jars with green beans, or sort mounds of soiled socks, grimy overalls, and ammonia-smelling diapers; but she knew a filly from a gelding and a roan from an Appaloosa. From hearing her speak of "people who really know horses," we knew that a person who "knew" horses was someone superior. We knew a steer from a heifer and an Angus from a Hereford, but didn't everyone?

Though I didn't know the story of why she didn't see her family, I had heard Snider's story. I'd asked one day, "When did you get Snider?" and the story came.

"Before I had Snider, I had a gray horse named Dan

that my dad had bought from Pete Morgan, who probably stole it. Pete always wanted that horse back and I guess he was mad cuz he couldn't have it. Then on the day of my grandmother Lindvall's funeral in 1931, Pete came into our barn and put acid under Dan's tail. After that, Dan was ruined. He became a tail switcher. A tail switcher just isn't dependable for riding."

Here my mother came out with one of her firm opinions. "That Pete Morgan. He was absolutely no good, but he would try to make out he was an honest man."

Her eyes sought the distant land, and her tone changed. "It's funny," she said, "how two people in the same family can be so different. Joe Morgan isn't like that."

We knew about the Morgans mostly because there were so many of them and because Joe's farm was such an eccentric place. Ephraim-like, the Morgans seemed to be related to everyone in the county. Joe must have applied the "multiply" directive to his machinery as well as to his family of twelve children. On his sprawling farm west on the Olson crossroad, row upon row of rusting, abandoned machinery spread over acres of land. I didn't know then how Joe Morgan had proven he "wasn't like that" in my parents' early married life.

Mama pushed aside thoughts of the Morgans and picked up her memories of Snider.

"Anyway, after that I took a milking shorthorn that I had—I bought that cow from Jim McLean—and my dad and I went to see Arnold Hanson, who had Snider for sale."

She described how she and her father planned to communicate about the black horse in front of the seller without sounding too eager and driving the price up. They agreed that if Grandpa Olson thought my mother should trade for the little black horse, he would tap on his snuff-box.

Well, my dad looked Snider over and tapped his snuff box so I got Snider. And my dad was right. I got a good horse. He's part mustang, you know, and that's why he isn't overly big. His mother ran with a wild mustang herd for awhile."

To my child's eyes, my mother's love and loyalty for Snider was like the intense feeling she obviously had for my father, but after her marriage, she was too housebound and too often sick to ride her beloved horse. In the early months of each pregnancy, Mama fought daily nausea; she had bouts with what we later learned were gall bladder attacks; she had two miscarriages in addition to delivering nine children.

When she was not feeling well, her love of talk lessened, and she temporarily lost interest in outside affairs. We couldn't count on fresh baked cookies every day when we came home from school, and she might not be at her accustomed four o'clock lunch time position next to my father at the table, where they took their time over coffee and the oatmeal cookies my father liked. Instead, she spent hours in her bedroom reading, trying to forget how bad she felt.

We children flaunted our lack of understanding. We complained about meals from a can, or about having to make supper ourselves. When we heard her throwing up in the bathroom, we joked about what a noisy "thrower-upper" she was, imitating her vocalized misery for greater effect.

My father didn't ride Snider either. One day at dinner, I asked him, "Why don't you ever ride Snider?"

He shrugged a silent response, but my mother's words were ready. "Well, you know, when Daddy was a boy, one of Grandpa's horses kicked him in the head. He had a headache for days. He can ride all right, though."

Daddy might not have been "someone who really knows horses," but Mama was proud of other talents he had, including his physical strength and his mechanical wizardry.

"Why, when Old Man Halskov did his threshing every fall, he always made sure he got Daddy to work for him. He said Daddy was as strong as three men. And Oscar Clementson put him in charge of stoking the threshing machine when he was just seventeen." When Mama bragged about her children, it embarrassed us, but we thought she just told the truth about Daddy. We, too, were proud of his strength, and that when all the fathers played baseball at our school's end-of-the-year picnic, Daddy seemed to run faster and throw better than the other fathers.

When my mother first had young children, she encouraged them to ride Snider, and she helped with the saddle and bridle. By the time I was a child, we sometimes rode Snider to bring the cows home for milking, but like our father, we didn't have Mama's knack or passion for riding, and we preferred less solitary activities. Snider spent most of his days alone, sharing our pastures with the Angus cattle. We thought of the herd of black cattle as belonging to my father, but the sturdy black horse with the white splotch on his forehead was only my mother's. To me, Snider was always an old horse. The only nonproductive animal on my frugal father's farm, he played no useful role in our practical world.

Like his mustang ancestors, Snider was tough and durable. Enduring the cold winters and the hot summers, he seemed a natural and permanent inhabitant of the unforgiving northern plains. To us, Snider was proof that my mother had once been someone else—a horsewoman, a rebellious

# This Storied Land

daughter, a teenager who bought a cow with money earned working for neighbors during hard times. He embodied the mysteries of her other life. When she married, my mother brought no linens or furniture or jewelry from her childhood home. She brought her horse.

On the Montana Hi-Line, the seasons march with pitiless tread, the sweeping treeless plains playing host to fierce battles. When I was seven, my parents decided to build a larger house, and that winter was the last the eight of us spent in our four-room homestead house. The winter came with a particularly triumphant step. Daily, my father struggled through swirling snow and cold to the barnyard, where he threw loosened hay bales to the gathered hungry livestock, seeing that Snider got his portion. To give the animals drink, he broke through the ice in the watering tank with the axe.

We fought our own winter battles inside our small house, a fox den protecting us from Nature. Sickness found our crowded pocket of warmth and visited us each in turn. My mother was pregnant with her seventh child and we heard few stories. Her characteristic smothered giggle rarely shook her softly padded frame.

One cold day, recovering from the measles or the flu or some childhood sickness, I rested on my mother's bed. From under a weight of blankets, I considered the sole decoration on my parents' bedroom wall, a wood-burning of a horse's head. Burned onto a plain wooden circle, the sparse dark lines projected a rebellious, untamed spirit. The horse's eyes were wild and wide; the nostrils flared and extravagantly burned coils formed the mane.

"Is that Snider?" I asked my mother.

"Sort of," she replied. A soft wistfulness showed in her eyes.

After such a winter, intimations of spring bring soaring feelings of liberation. Our winter-white faces lifted to feel the warm chinook wind. The snow began to melt. We found a bare, dry spot on the driveway to turn a jump-rope braided from baler twine. Even my father joined us for a few minutes, swinging one end of the long rope, his head thrown back, laughing. In Hunter School, the teacher celebrated the end of winter with a list on the blackboard titled "Signs of Spring." Each day she added a new sign of spring, followed by the name of the child who first reported that herald of the new season. First was "Crocus—Jerry Johnson." Next, "Meadowlark—Sharon Goltz." Then, "Ducks flying—John Houth."

By April, our blue-skyed world was full of the south wind, a wind which rid the prairie of winter, drying the mud, coaxing green out of the brown landscape, encouraging my mother to hang the wash on the outside clothesline and throw open the windows. The cattle left the manure-packed barnyard to search out newly uncovered prairie grass.

On one of those days when the south wind was driving out winter, my mother stopped suddenly as she carried a load of just-washed diapers out to the line. Dropping the clothesbasket, she straightened and pointed with delighted triumph. "Look!" Just beyond the clothesline lay a section of pasture where Snider was racing across the land like a yearling, head high, black mane and tail flying, hooves swift and sure. My mother laughed, a real laugh, not her more usual half-suppressed giggle. She walked close to the fence surrounding the pasture, and I watched the woman and her horse. The horse's shaggy coat was a reminder of the hard winter, but his body stood solid and sturdy, a testimony to his enduring strength. The woman had graying hair and a body rounded by giving and sustaining life, but that day she was more than what I saw.

For a moment the woman I saw was not my mother. She had a kinship with this horse that I couldn't know. Both were cut off from their past, my mother from her childhood family, the horse from his kind. But both stood surely on the warming prairie earth, more clearly a sign of spring than anything listed on the blackboard at school. Watching the strong, clean wind blow her hair and his mane, I thought of the picture of them in the desk drawer and the wood-burning on my parents' bedroom wall. I felt an aching loss I couldn't understand.

lou mandler

# Four

# The Invisible Family

Just on the other side of the elms, Russian olives, caraganas, and chokecherry trees in the east shelterbelt, a gravel road curved past our house. We could sit at table, on the front step, or in the front room (as we called our living room) and watch the vehicles traveling north to Hunter or south, where fifteen miles of gravel road and highway led to Plentywood (simply "town" to us). There Daddy bought our groceries and supplies. The road connected us to school and town and our neighbors. Lined in the summer with brome grass, perfumed yellow sweet clover, and occasional clumps of wild sunflowers, this north-south corridor bore little traffic, but we watched that traffic closely.

We knew the wood-paneled station wagon belonging to the Hunter depot agent, Bob Durbin; we knew the old black pickup of our bachelor neighbor, Leonard Norman; the sundry Morgan vehicles; and the red truck and large Chevy sedan belonging to Helmer Halvorsen and Orville Gronvold, farmers between Hunter and the Canadian line. The occasional truck, pickup, or car passing by told us who had started harvest, who went to town often, and who was selling wheat at the elevators in Hunter.

We watched one unusual truck extra closely. Its owner had painted the head of a bull on the side of the truck box, highlighted in bright tones of yellow and red. It wasn't just that no one else sported a colorful sign on the side of his truck. This sign announced with a flourish, "Carl Olson. Registered Shorthorns." Carl Olson was my mother's brother, the uncle I had never seen.

Our glimpses of this truck and driver reminded us of everything we didn't know about our mother's family. We did know my mother's younger sister Emily, her husband Hans, and their children, but by the time I was six, they had moved to Kalispell in the western part of the state. We didn't know why my mother maintained a warm relationship with her sister but neither spoke to nor saw her brother and her parents. By the time I was old enough to know this mystery existed, asking about it was an unspoken taboo.

We burned with curiosity about Carl and our grandparents. We knew what they looked like from the photos in the picture drawer, taken before the silence started. Looking at these photos was not forbidden, but looking was all we felt free to do.

# This Storied Land

My Grandfather Olson was immediately recognizable in the pictures because of the sunken place where his left eye should have been. The silence surrounding the subject of our grandparents was so deep that we didn't ask why he was maimed in this way. Not until I was an adult did I learn how, when my mother was nine years old, her father lost his eye.

He had placed a bent iron rod on a rock to steady it as he straightened the metal. As he hammered, a small piece of rock flew up and became embedded in his eye. He borrowed a buckboard and drove to the doctor, but the doctor's attention and a subsequent surgery failed to save the eye. He later went by train to Minot, where another doctor removed it. We children discussed the fact that in his photos, Grandpa Olson was not a big smiler. He looked sad, we thought.

In those pictures, my Grandma Olson's image was remarkable for her arresting cloud of hair, white even at the age of thirty, and for her lively look. The eyes that shone from her likenesses in the picture drawer seemed brimming with questions and comments. She looked as if she had stopped talking and moving just long enough for the click of the camera to take place. The suggestion of an active, determined mind reminded me of my own mother. Later we learned that it was Grandma Olson who had snapped many of the photos we owned, including the one of Snider and my mother. By the time I knew this, I could also understand that Grandma Olson's obsession with picture-taking was a natural outgrowth of her fascination with people, her high energy, and her interest in whatever was new.

So we knew what our grandparents looked like, but not what they were like in life. Grandma Olson was the one who really piqued our interest. Her image and her name always seemed to evoke intensely negative feelings in my mother. Despite her refusal to speak about her mother, Mama was clearly embarrassed by and ashamed of her. We strove to supply reasons for this feeling. One day as my brother Arthur and I rode in the hayrack behind the tractor, balancing with flexed knees and spread feet, our conversation turned to our invisible relatives.

"Have you ever seen Grandma Olson?" I asked him.

"Yes," he said. "I've seen her once or twice in town."

I was excited. "What was she like, what do you think she *is* like?" I asked.

"Well, I think she is probably the kind of woman who, if she itched anywhere, would scratch it," he said.

This critical observation roughly fit with the impression I had formed, based on the very few comments my mother had made over the years. Once I began reading a letter aloud to her, and she burst out, "Don't do that! My ma used to get the mail and start reading it out loud before we got a chance to read it for ourselves." Another time, she referred to her mother with an air of disgust: "Oh, she's a wild one, all right." So the image I had of my grandmother was of an impulsive, active, talkative woman who could never be described as refined.

My mother gave few hints of her feelings for her father, but she talked sometimes of his relatives in Minnesota, people who seemed successful, friendly. When, much later, I learned that my mother was her father's favorite, I felt an aching wonder at the years of silence between them.

Our Uncle Carl was the third unknown. In the photos, he was tall and spectacled. His bony face always showed a half smile under his disheveled, curly hair. My first real-life encounter with my Uncle Carl was a gift of the weather, of one cold winter night as my father and I drove home from town. Darkness fell early these winter days. Although, by the clock, it was not yet truly evening, no trace of daylight remained; the sky was cloudless, and the stars fully exposed so the world was just snow, sky, stars. Our car with my father and me inside was just a bump on the land. The winter night had a blue cast, the color of loneliness.

After turning north onto the gravel road from the highway, we had traveled a couple of miles when we saw a stalled pickup in the road ahead. In this country, on this road, it was unthinkable not to stop, especially in this cold. My father left our old Buick running and approached the man working under the raised hood of the stalled pickup. As he and my father spoke to each other, each uttered word sent a puff of white into the cold air. Soon my father returned to our car and waited as the stranded man continued trying to start his vehicle.

"Who is that?" I asked, surprised that my father had not stayed out in the cold to help the man. My father loved a mechanical puzzle. There was a silence as we waited. I was used to pauses when talking with my father, but this pause was longer than most.

Finally, in a surprised tone, he said, "You don't know who that is?"

"No."

Another pause.

"Why, that's Carl Olson," he finally said but added nothing more.

My uncle soon had his motor going, and he drove away. My father and I continued on our way under the blue-black sky and the cold bright stars. Now that Carl Olson had turned off the road, we were alone in the night. We didn't speak again in the last miles to home. I wondered what my father was thinking, wondered if he would tell my mother about their daughter who didn't recognize her uncle. I was embarrassed and sad.

I was a middle-aged woman when I told this story to my sisters and brother. My sister Vivien responded with a story of her own. She was in the office at the high school one day when a tall man with glasses, a crooked smile, and curly, unruly hair walked in and spoke to the secretary.

"I'm here to pay for a month's lunch tickets for my daughter, Marjorie Olson," she heard him say.

My sister realized that she was in the same room as her uncle. He gave no sign of knowing who she was.

And then Arthur told of a time when he was a young boy, and my father was looking for some cattle who had escaped our pastures. He and Arthur drove to the Olsons, and my father sent Arthur to the door to inquire about our lost cattle while Daddy waited in the car. It wasn't until he returned to the car that he learned it was his uncle who lived in the house and answered the door.

Such glimpses of our close relatives served to stoke our curiosity and made us impatient with our parents' secretiveness, but we felt paralyzed to pierce the shell of silence.

Despite the lack of contact with our mother's family, we were always aware of the existence of her parents and her brother and his family. Their farm in the hollow only four miles from ours was a place shrouded in mystery for us, peopled by close relatives who were stranger to us than our worldly neighbors.   Snider, grazing alone in our pasture, served as a symbol of my mother's other family.  We sensed that the passion causing the estrangement in our family seemed rooted in the women—our gritty mother, our colorful grandmother, matched strength for strength.  Our mother never rolled her eyes or grimaced with disgust when the subject of her father came up, so we guessed the mild-mannered men— our father, our grandfather—were bystanders.

lou mandler

# Five

# First Grace

Religion was paired with food when it first entered my life. It was an early summer evening when I was five. We five "big kids," glorying in how the June sky held onto the sun until nearly bedtime, were playing a shriek-filled game of tag in the yard. My mother was preparing a late farm supper inside our white clapboard house, the same house in which Jens Ibsen had lived. The cramped inside space of lean-to kitchen; central small front room with adjacent bedroom; and the enclosed porch, serving as my parents' bedroom; drew us outside to play whenever possible.

At 8:30 p.m., the farmer's suppertime, our mother

called us. "Hey, kids, time to eat!" As usual, we stole another few minutes for our game of tag amidst the ragweed and gravel in our hard dirt yard. The next call was impatient. "Suppertime! Now or never!"

We tumbled into the kitchen. Our father was already seated at his end of the table. It was he, not my mother, who would demand, "Let's see those hands!" if he saw us pass by the wash pan in the corner of the kitchen.

My mother had laid the table and dished up our usual meal of homemade bread, boiled potatoes, home-canned vegetables, and beef. The white enamel pitcher, full of milk from our Holstein cows, sat in the middle of the table during this and all the meals of my childhood.

We took our places, Agnes in the middle on one side of the table, my little sister Betsy and Arthur on either side of her; on the other side, my sister Diana sat in the middle with Vivien on one side and me on the other. Eyes on the food, we were poised to receive our share of the meal. We were always alert while the food held out. When you shared your meals with several hungry siblings, you couldn't afford to be dreamy. I once burst into tears when I didn't get my share of canned creamed corn.

I reached for a slice of bread. My mother, who was sitting next to me, grasped my arm and placed my hand in my lap. At the same time, my father said, "Just a minute," to my brother, who had tried to attack the plate of sliced roast beef. I glanced around the table. What was this? My parents said nothing more but waited for quiet. They had puzzled us into speechlessness. Seizing the silence, and with no explanation, Mama and Daddy bowed their heads and my father spoke a table grace of his own words, a grace we were to hear regularly over the years:

"Our Father, we thank thee for this food . . ."

That first supper with a grace was a quieter meal than usual. Questions about this new practice bubbled in our minds, but we didn't voice them. My father's mostly silent presence restrained us. He was good at many things, but not at talking. If we pestered him with questions, we knew by now to expect certain standard responses. We knew, too, what his short statements really meant. "Oh, I don't know" was likely to turn into a "No, I don't think so." A "We'll see" promised a much more positive outcome. "Oh, never mind" meant it was none of our business or that our question embarrassed him.

Daddy hoarded his sentences as though they were barrels of precious rainwater. He rarely uttered more than a sentence at a time. We accepted his word-parsimony without complaint. We were used to it. My father's delayed, one sentence method of giving information frustrated us only if my mother, his complement, was not around.


One such time occurred three years after our first supper with grace, the morning after my little sister Lillian, the seventh child, was born. We weren't surprised when my mother was not at breakfast that morning because the night before she had been in the bedroom packing a bag. We had eaten supper without her. My father cooked the hot oatmeal for our breakfast, and we sat at our usual places. He said grace. Using a wooden spoon, his big hands dished the oatmeal into enamel bowls, and we began eating. As we ate, we watched him, waiting. He ate methodically, head down, looking at his food, not speaking. We did as he did and spooned up the hot cereal, silently, but we exchanged looks and squirmed in our chairs. Mama's empty place made this meal strange; the unannounced news in the air and the silence made it nearly unbearable. Finally, some of us gave up the waiting game and started to push back our chairs to leave the table. My father cleared his throat.

"Well," he said, "You have a new baby sister."


By the time we sat down to our first supper with grace, we had learned long ago that our father was not comfortable playing the role of the herald. Our mother sat at the other end of the table as always, but she, too, kept a deliberate quiet. Having such a father cultivated patience in his children. We waited for the relaxed time after supper when Daddy had left the table to read or nap in the front room.

As soon as we were alone at table with my mother, we shot questions at her. "Why did Daddy say grace tonight?" She reminded us of what my older brother and sister must have understood, that she and Daddy had "professed," or chosen to live in The Truth, at the convention we had all attended for the last few days. "We decided that we should start going to meeting like Grandpa and Grandma and Uncle Barney and Aunt Tillie do."

Daddy's Uncle Barney and his wife Tillie lived nearer than any of my father's other relatives, a journey of an hour and a half. We visited them occasionally and knew about The Truth, their religion. Grandpa and Grandma Wiedeman's visits to our farm from their home in Washington State had also familiarized us with the ways of The Truth. The people

# This Storied Land

in The Truth not only lived differently and worshipped differently; they also looked different from "worldly" people.

Like all women in The Truth, Grandma Wiedeman and Aunt Tillie wore their gray hair long, following the admonition of the Apostle Paul in his letter to the Corinthians, "But if a woman have long hair, it is a glory to her; for her hair is given her for a covering." They rolled, twisted, braided, or wrapped their hair and then pinned it on the top or the back of their heads. Professing people took literally the advice in Paul's letter to Timothy, ". . . women must adorn themselves in modest apparel, with shamefacedness and sobriety. . ." In my memory, all the women in The Truth wear small-print floral dresses with long sleeves and gathered skirts. The men in The Truth wear ordinary dress shirts and slacks, rarely ornate cowboy clothes. Everyone looks scrubbed clean.

The spiritual highlight of the year for professing people was the convention we had just attended. It was also the social highlight of the year for those in The Truth. More than three hundred people attended the four-day June convention on a farm thirty miles south of our farm. Families came from three hundred miles away and attended three meetings each day, Thursday through Sunday.

To my five-year-old eyes, our first convention was a thrilling, sense-filled experience, interspersed with intolerably long sermon-and-prayer-filled meetings. As we turned from the gravel road into the farmyard for convention, I saw a farm transformed into a scene that suggested a country fair or one of the auction sales my father loved. Row upon row of cars filled a hayfield near the road. Clusters of men and women stood visiting in the farmyard. Small children raced about.

## lou mandler

When my father had parked our car and we, too, entered the farmyard, I knew this was no fair or auction sale. As the hour for the morning meeting neared, the knots of visiting people, black Bibles and hymn books in hand, headed for the huge machine shed. Inside this shed-turned-meeting hall, the damp smell of the sand-covered dirt floor pervaded the air. Sitting on hard plank benches, we survived the two-hour meetings by scribbling in the notebooks my mother had provided and periodically sucking on Lifesavers. The words the ministers or "workers" spoke from the platform made little impression on me at my first convention.

As soon as the meetings ended, the fun part of convention began. With the clang of a bell, men, women, and children crowded into the barn-turned-whitewashed-dining room. Here too, sand covered the dirt floor. The farm families that attended brought the food for convention meals, prepared in a kitchen off the dining hall barn. During mealtime, the dining hall rang with the clang and thump of metal pans of boiled potatoes and stew against the white plank tables. The sweet tang of rhubarb desserts and the spicy breakfast hash are, to me, mixed up with the rising and falling inflections of preaching and prayer.

Being at convention was like camping out, but better. With dozens of others, ranging from children to women in their fifties, we slept on straw-filled ticks in the big hayloft of the barn. The old ladies and the women with babies slept in separate tents pitched near the meeting shed. On our farm, bound together by talk, isolation, and shared space and activities, we Wiedeman children shared an identity. Now, for the first time, we felt part of a group outside our family. We felt part of a very good thing; we felt neat and clean and right inside.

The last meeting of a convention, on Sunday night, was always a Gospel meeting, a service designed to make people repent and seek salvation. It gave them an opportunity to profess or become part of The Truth. This was not a religion of yelling, "Praise the Lord." Except for occasional quiet weeping, emotion was always restrained. When the Gospel Meeting was "tested" at convention the year I was five, my parents professed. While the gathering sang the last verse and chorus of a hymn, . . . *Hear Him now, calling you, Do not turn from Him away:/ Give Him room in your heart, Let Him guide you ev'ry day*, my parents rose to their feet and remained standing until the last note of the hymn had sounded. With that simple action, my mother and father formally declared their intention to live in The Truth. And so my father said our first grace at supper that June evening.

Our daily lives didn't change much after my parents professed. My father's family had been in The Truth since he was twelve, and he saw to it that his young family followed the principle of The Truth to be "in the world but not of the world." Even before my parents stood up that day, we had never partaken in what the world sees as entertainment. Card playing or gambling of any kind, drinking alcohol, smoking, dancing, movies, and television, when it became available, were worldly pleasures we knew nothing of. Celebrations of Christmas and Easter were not included in our seasonal cycles. Despite The Truth's disapproval of females wearing male clothing, we continued to wear blue jeans at home. Skirts just didn't work for hauling hay or riding bike or bringing the cattle home for milking. Besides, a good pair of jeans would last all summer. We did not, however, wear jeans to town, and my mother never wore jeans. For my father, to profess was simply to affirm the religion of his childhood.

For my mother, however, to profess was to abandon consciously and openly the Lutheran religion in which she had been confirmed. Years later, she told me that her father once said to her, "I would sooner see you in your grave than see you not be a Lutheran." Among the stash of photographs in the desk drawer, one shows my mother in a white dress on a windy day. It was taken on her Confirmation Day, and she is wearing a corsage and holding a Bible in her hand. For us, this image commemorating our mother's participation in a Lutheran ceremony gave her an intriguing, but somewhat shameful, aura of worldliness, documenting a past of which we knew almost nothing. We never doubted that it was my mother's choice to join my father in following his religion, but about this decision she told no stories. Her life as a Lutheran was definitely a closed chapter of her life, mysterious to us children.

What was new for us after our first supper with grace was that we began going to Sunday morning meetings in the home of the Petersons, an older couple who lived about six miles south of our home. The content of the meetings—the hymn singing, prayer, and testimonies from the professing people—was not always interesting to us, but like young anthropologists, we carefully examined everyone's expressions, gestures, and physical traits. As the glass of grape juice and the crustless piece of white bread passed from hand to hand during communion, we covertly watched its progress around the room, noticing who gulped and who sipped. Calm and quiet reigned at these Sunday morning meetings. Fellowship, not conversion, was the goal; thankfulness and humility, not potential damnation, was the common theme. When meeting was over, everyone shook hands all around, and afterward we children discussed even the quality of people's handshakes. Old Man Barsness's huge hands were warm, frail Grandma Swenson's shake was weak, friendly Gordon Peterson's was brisk and firm.

We had not visited many other homes, and we gazed, marveling, at the neatness of the Petersons' household. We had never before seen such a neatly made bed with the chenille spread pulled so tightly over the pillows. Somehow Mrs. Peterson's uncluttered living room, her polished kitchen floor and gleaming appliances came to be joined in my mind with the spick and span feeling of being right with God and being amongst His Chosen People. The aroma of the beef roasting in her oven filled the air as we listened to the Word of God. These kind and neat people coming together in a perfectly kept home believed they were in the straight and narrow Way that led to God's Truth. This ordered, calm world was appealing. It felt right and safe.

With his measured manner and speech, our father seemed to fit into the culture of the Sunday morning meeting. But our mother was not the mother we knew at home. At meeting she was almost always careful, watchful, circumspect. At home she was relaxed, brutally honest, quick with retorts, laughter, and admonishments. In neither place had she learned how to agree just to be nice. We thought Mama behaved pretty well when we went to Sunday morning meeting, but we worried that her irrepressible frankness and the delight she took in surprising or mildly shocking people might break out and embarrass us.

Being part of The Truth made us different from our

neighbors. In the manner of The Truth, we didn't socialize with nonprofessing people. In fact, we saw and spoke with people outside our family only through school, meeting, and going to town. We were our own society, watched over by our father and mother, figures whose different natures worked together to balance our little society. But it wasn't just The Truth that made us different. That picture of my mother in her Confirmation clothes and the pictures of her parents reminded us that our family had secrets.

# This Storied Land

lou mandler

# Six

# Last Meeting

I was in the third grade when my sister Diana broke her arm playing softball at Hunter School. My father drove her the fifteen miles to Plentywood in our maroon Kaiser, and the doctor set her arm. When they came home, he brought tragic news involving the Barsnesses, a family in The Truth, who had been neighbors of my father's family when he was a boy.

The elder Barsnesses had professed at the same time my grandparents had. Melvin, their son, who was near my father's age, now lived with his dark-haired, vivacious wife Evelyn and their three children on a farm south of town.

The news my father brought back from Plentywood was that Melvin and Evelyn's youngest child, three-year-old Daniel, had been crushed to death under the wheels of the family truck. Few farm families escaped living with the remorse resulting from an injury or death caused by a few seconds of inattention or carelessness. The Petersons' young granddaughter had lost an arm in the grain auger; one of the Morgans had lost a couple of fingers in the rock picker; Leonard Norman had a wooden leg; a teen-aged boy working his uncle's field a few miles west of us caught a tractor wheel on a large rock, and when the tractor tipped over, he was pinned beneath it and killed. My mother's left leg was slightly shorter and thinner than her right leg, a reminder of an accident when, at age ten, she fell out of the family buggy on the way to town. The buggy wheel ran over her leg and broke it.

But in counting the painful regrets involved in all accidents, the death of little Daniel Barsness cut sharper, harder, deeper because he was only three. Because the father was driving the truck that crushed his son.

The day of Daniel's death, we had been watching the south road for my father and sister's arrival from town, and as soon as the car stopped outside the entryway, we leapt to meet them. Excited by this novel visit to the doctor, we hurled questions at my sister.

"Diana, what was it like?"

"Did it hurt when he put the cast on?"

"Is that thing heavy?"

"Can you still play tag?"

We didn't bother to glance at my father who went wordlessly into the house. Still chattering and excited, we swept inside like a small beehive on alert, Diana in our midst as Queen Bee. My father and mother were standing in front of the window by the stove, their backs to the room. We continued ministering to our Queen Bee and hardly noticed when my father left the kitchen and went outside. It would be up to my mother, the one who talked, to decide whether and how to tell us about the death of a child we knew.

My mother's stories often had no introductions. Now, her death announcement was just that, an announcement, pure and unadorned. Once the buzz of first interest over Diana's cast had stilled, my mother spoke into the lull.

"Daniel Barsness was killed today. He was run over by a truck. Daddy will be going to the funeral."

And so the unimaginable occurs. Our reality reeled for days.

We never thought that Daddy's silence meant he had nothing to say. We took in his actions, his observant eyes, a scowl, the lift of an eyebrow, a lifted head, a brow knit in thought, the sudden, unexpected laugh with his head thrown back, and we accepted that Daddy was smart and kind. We just didn't know exactly what he thought. In the days following Daniel's death, he was absolutely silent and closed, present only physically, and I finally, thoughtlessly, asked my mother,

"What's wrong with Daddy, anyway?"

Because of my mother's separation from her family and her isolation on the farm, we heard stories that other women probably told only to their friends and adult relatives. This was one of the times when a question poked a hole in the dyke that held in my mother's ruminating, and her answer sounded like the beginning of a story.

"Oh, of course he's upset about Daniel's accident. Just think how awful it must be for Melvin to have killed his own son. But I think, too, that it brings back other bad memories. For one thing, it probably makes him think of when his sister Elsie died."

We knew Daddy's little sister had died when she was five and he was ten, but that's all we knew. I probed.

"And how did she die?"

Mama said it was probably a case of meningitis. Elsie got sick in the fall, just as it was turning winter. My mother said at first Grandpa and Grandma Wiedeman thought it was just the flu, but Elsie got steadily worse until she was so ill that Grandpa Wiedeman made a rush trip to Wildrose to get the doctor.

"When they got back to the house, the doctor couldn't do a thing, and she died with the doctor and the family in the room," my mother said.

I tried to imagine my father telling my mother about this sad time. He was just five years older than little Elsie, and Mama said that after she died, he missed her dreadfully. My mother stopped her story and worked her mouth for a while. Then she continued.

"Grandpa Wiedeman told me about her death once. He told me that when Elsie died, he was holding her in his arms. I can remember exactly what he said, 'She was lying there in my arms when all of a sudden she gave a start, she gasped, and then she went limp. I will carry the feeling of that little body in my arms until the day I die.'"

My mother paused again, and we pondered that long-ago tragedy together. But she had more on her mind.

"Poor Daddy. He has seen some terrible things

happen. And he's so sensitive."

We believed that my father was sensitive, but it was difficult to know whether we saw it for ourselves or whether we believed it because my mother said so. I waited.

"You know, another thing that happened was when his cousin Arthur died. He and Daddy were the same age and they got along really well. Barney and Tillie's sons, Arthur and his brother, had bleeder's disease, you know. They always had to be very careful not to get hurt or they could bleed to death. And in those days there wasn't much doctors could do about it. Well, one December day Daddy and Arthur went out rabbit hunting. Everything seemed fine, but the next day Arthur was sick, and it turned out he had somehow moved wrong or fallen or something while they were hunting to cause internal hemorrhaging. Well, they couldn't do anything, and Arthur was dead in a few days."

I was slowly grasping the obvious while my mother spoke.

"So you named Arthur after Arthur Pieper?" I asked. She nodded.

The week Daniel died we did not go to Sunday morning meeting with our usual appetite for people-watching. Melvin and Evelyn Barsness would be in our meeting, and we felt the awkwardness and sorrow that comes from being in the presence of a grief that cannot be assuaged. As the meeting began, its established order—the opening hymn, the community prayers—provided a sense of security and comfort for us. Then it was time for testimonies. Jim Peterson spoke. My father spoke. Two or three others rose to their feet and gave their thoughts on a Bible verse that had meant something to them as they read their Bible in private that week.    Finally Evelyn Barsness stood, Bible in hand. She began speaking, successfully struggling for control. We children gaped, marveling.    She had uttered barely three sentences before she stopped, fought tears through the next sentence, and then abruptly sat down and gave way to wrenching sobs. We gaped again, chilled to the heart.

I don't remember discussing this scene at home. Although my older siblings went to meeting regularly after they left home, it was the last meeting my father went to for scores of years.    Not until he was seventy did he begin attending Sunday morning meetings again. The crazy zigzag between stories and silences in which we lived didn't give us an answer for his years of absence. Was it a loss of faith after a cruel accident to an innocent boy?    Or did this accident or this particular meeting revive some shadow in my father's heart?    Whatever the cause, from then on we lived in a religious borderland, circumscribed by silence. As we didn't ask Mama about her family, so we didn't ask Daddy why we didn't go to meeting.

For a time, Daddy continued to say grace before meals, but in a few years his spoken grace was replaced by a time of silence as we bowed our heads.    Sunday mornings, too, became an unnaturally quiet time, filled with our awareness that we were removed from the world and from The Truth. Our father never did farm work on Sundays, our mother never did laundry or other heavy chores, and we girls never cleaned the house or worked in the garden.    We had time to think about the quiet on Sunday morning.    Our family followed the restrictions of life in The Truth, and my father brought us to Convention once a year.    But we were really outsiders.    After the last meeting, we were our own society

# This Storied Land

more than ever, ruled by my parents and the wind and the sky
and the seasons of the land.

lou mandler

# Seven

# The World of Hunter

Because we went to school in Hunter, we became acquainted with its residents. In going to school, we also began to know something about the world.

Hunter lay just under two miles north of our farm by the gravel road. Sometimes we walked to school. Sometimes we rode bicycles. Sometimes my father took us. Hunter School was on a grassy hill, surrounded on three sides by wheat fields and on the north by a small grove of hardy maple and caragana trees, planted as all trees were in this country by a long-ago optimist. Our school had been built as the high school, but after 1938, high school students went to school in

Plentywood, and the Hunter High School became simply Hunter School. A gigantic tuba and other abandoned equipment in the storage room and the books for older students in the library continued to remind us that our school had first been a high school.

From the hilltop on the south edge of this greatly diminished little town, the school looked over the remnants of Hunter's former pride. The banks, the cigar factory, and the stores of the 1920s were gone; some had burned, some had been torn down, some had fallen down. By the time we went to school, few buildings remained. The Soo Line still employed an agent, Mrs. Kennedy, who lived upstairs in the yellow depot next to the railroad tracks on the north edge of town. Two great grain elevators loomed west of the depot, and the post office, also home to the Houth family, marked the center of Hunter. A time-worn, white frame church stood, graying and abandoned, on the road east to Rostad. Between the Houth home and the church, the square, windowless jail was still in good repair. A gravel road with three right-angle turns, unique in this country of straight roads, wound through Hunter and then several miles straight north to the Canadian border.

Henry Larsson and his Indian wife Maria lived just east of the Hunter post office in a weathered, unwelcoming house. Henry often drove past our farm on his way home from Plentywood. His black '48 coupe weaving, "Ole Henry" maneuvered the gravel road through the alcoholic haze he had gone to town to acquire. Certainly it was my mother's sympathy for Maria and her children, not her disgust with Ole Henry, that once persuaded my parents to allow Maria's husband to park his black coupe for a couple weeks behind our barn. They never told us why the car had to be hidden. Even today my best guess is that the county sheriff had an eye out for it. My mother's fierce loyalty to Maria Larsson contrasted to the more negative way others in the community viewed its Indian residents. We saw this as just another way my mother was different from our neighbors.

Besides the Houths, Mrs. Kennedy, and the Larssons, the other people who lived in Hunter were the Johnsons, the Doyles, and Leonard Norman. After Leonard Norman, we knew the Houths and the Doyles best because we went to school with Marie Doyle and John Houth.

The Houths ran the only two businesses in Hunter, the grain elevators and the post office. They also farmed a few hundred acres. Their two-story house with a front porch was by far the nicest of the few houses in Hunter. Their house contained the post office in the space just off the front parlor, and once in a while, we were allowed to get the mail. We loved entering the post office through its separate door, ringing the bell, and waiting for Norma Houth to come from her kitchen, bedroom, or who knew where to look at us through the grated window and push our mail out to us. She never appeared without wearing bright red lipstick. Her strong-boned face was pleasant, but not quick to smile. Norma Houth had learned her housekeeping tasks thoroughly at Indian boarding school, and she kept an immaculate house. She dressed in tailored slacks and smart blouses, and her jet-black hair was well coifed. Unlike my mother and most other farm wives, she carried no extra flesh on her small frame.

Raymond Houth, the tallest man in the Hunter country, usually wore blue jeans and a western shirt, not the overalls and chambray work shirts that my father and other farmers wore. To us, Raymond's most fascinating quality was not his lean frame or dark eyes, but his unusual hissing laugh. When he was amused, he opened his lips, keeping his teeth closed, and the forced air of his laughter hissed through his closed teeth. Raymond's cheekbones were so sharp that I imagined them creasing his pillow. When the Houths went in to town to the meetings of the Sheridan Saddle Club, they wore fancy tooled boots, dress cowboy hats, and ornate leather belts.

Although Marie Doyle started grade one with my sister Agnes, by the time I was in school, she was two years behind Agnes, in the same grade as my sister Vivien. Our family did not have enough to waste, but the Doyles seemed to have even less than we did. Only the unpainted boards of Newton and Nova's flimsy shack separated the one room and an entry from the outdoors. The entry also contained an open cistern from which the Doyles took their water. Newton had spent years digging coal, building elevators, cleaning out a livery barn—working at any job he could find. Then he worked on the Soo Line as a section worker, maintaining the railroad. Newton was a tough giant of a man, and his years on the railroad had given him hardened muscles and a colorful vocabulary.

Because Newton and Nova never owned a car, Nova caught rides into Plentywood with Leonard Norman to buy groceries. Nova wore floral dresses, never pants, and she arranged her dark, waist-length hair coiled over her ears in the 1920s hair fashion known then as "cootie garages." The Mona Lisa smile below her dark, interested eyes nearly masked the fact that Nova had no teeth. When I was in high school, I discovered that she nourished a shelf-full of flourishing houseplants and embroidered pillow cases and dresser scarves. The sheets on her clothesline were as white as the neighbors' sheets. But we didn't know that when we were younger. Then, we only knew that other Hunter women looked with disapproval on Nova's housekeeping. We had heard the scornful talk about her household clutter and uncleanness from girls at school.

Skinny, dark-haired, freckled, and uninhibited, Marie was the youngest of Newton and Nova Doyle's five living children. Four other babies Nova had borne lay in tiny graves in the little cemetery in Hunter. Marie often walked home with my sisters after school. She taught us to look for agates mixed in with the gravel on the road as we walked. Lively and talkative, she certainly sought the company of my sisters, but the fresh baked cookies my mother usually had ready for the arrival of her school kids must also have enticed Marie.

We learned news of Marie's family on the walks between school and our farm. We knew when her brother David married Helen, a German girl who had endured the hardships of the war in Germany and at eighteen had come to northern Montana alone as a post-war refugee, sponsored by an aunt. We were sad with Marie when David and Helen's first son died soon after birth. We were happy with her when they had a healthy son the following fall.

Then one spring week, Helen was in school with us. Our teacher, Mr. Jensen, had agreed that if she attended for a week, he would help her prepare for the citizenship test. By then, Helen was the twenty-year-old mother of an infant son, but at four foot ten inches, she was shorter than all the sixth, seventh, and eighth-graders. She spent her school days with us learning about the United States government and improving her English. Nova Doyle cared for her grandson while Helen was in school.

One day that week, Helen stood in front of our classroom and spoke to all the students in our school about life in Germany. She talked about how strict German teachers were, of how one of them walked down the aisle one day slapping each student on the hands. She walked part-way down our own aisle, gesturing to left and right. I shivered. When she described how the teachers made the students clean the schools, my brother Arthur decided that Germany must have been a terrible place.

We couldn't understand why a grown woman would choose to come to school for a week. But her story gave us an inkling of why she was determined to become an American citizen, and it made us think about what we Americans take for granted.

At ten, Helen had left her mother to go to school in the city. She'd had no real home again until she married David Doyle in Montana when she was eighteen. She told us that as the war intensified, she and her sister got on the last train out of eastern Germany. She was lifted onto the train through a window, and the car was so crowded that at first her feet didn't touch the floor. Her sister soon went on to Heidelberg, but Helen lived, an unwelcome guest, wherever authorities sent her. At the war's end, a couple who had lost their son wanted to adopt her. "But I cried and begged to go to my sister," she said.

An unwanted refugee, she spoke of a fear and anger we had never known. "Soldiers with bayonets came into the house where I lived. They slashed the feather beds, cut the

# This Storied Land

belt on the sewing machine, and smashed things," she said. People turned dogs on her. She was constantly hungry after the war. I tried to imagine not having meat and garden vegetables to eat.

I learned later that when Helen arrived at her aunt's home in June of 1950, she could speak only limited English. She spent the summer improving her English by reading her aunt's supply of *Life* magazines.

And so it was that Hunter School brought some of the world into our lives, not only through books but through those who came to northern Montana from elsewhere.

lou mandler

# Eight

# The Teacher from Phoenix

Even the best teachers stayed in Hunter only a year. We first saw Miss Tucker, my first-grade teacher, when she walked into our yard one late summer day as we children played near where our father was greasing the combine. Although we sometimes walked home from school, we rarely saw other walkers on the gravel road that passed our farm. Anyone on foot was usually in search of help for a broken-down vehicle on the road. But on this day no vehicle was in sight. The slender, dark-haired woman entering our yard wore nylon stockings and dress shoes. Even my father stopped his work to witness her arrival.

# lou mandler

"Well! It's the new teacher," he said in surprise. This summer one of the ads listing Hunter's teaching position had brought a response from a teacher in Arizona, and the deal had been consummated through the mail. Miss Tucker had arrived in Hunter two days before on the passenger car of the Soo Line, and my father, who was the clerk of the school board, had brought her to the school and the one-room "teacherage" (as the spartan housing for rural teachers was called) in which she would live for a year. He had given her a contract to sign and return. And now Miss Pearl Tucker, a single woman in her fifties from Phoenix, Arizona, was marching over the dry ruts and parched weeds in our yard, unruffled by the curious gaze of my father and five of his children. She stopped in front of him and, not bothering with pleasantries, got to the point.

"I brought my contract," she said. "May I see your copy?"

In the two minutes that it took my father to secure his copy from the house, Miss Tucker and her future students examined each other. We saw a fierce-looking woman whose penetrating dark eyes had lost none of their spark on the dusty, two-mile walk she had just completed. Her thin flyaway hair was cut short, and later we speculated that she dyed it. All together, her black hair, dress, dark lipstick, and confident carriage spoke "city." She saw four girls and a boy huddled together, staring at her in astonishment. Our girls' braids and my brother's home haircut, our hightop brown shoes and cotton dresses, and my brother's overalls all said "farm." Just then my father returned and offered her a folded piece of paper. Miss Tucker took it, and swiftly tore both copies of the contract into several pieces.

Our mouths fell open. My father's eyebrows went up

as he started forward to retrieve the pieces. But Miss Tucker had not fulfilled her mission.

"Look," she said. "I'm here, and I will teach in your school this year. I said I would, and I will. I don't need a contract for that. But I did not agree to start the stove every morning as it says here. I don't know anything about oil stoves. And I am not a janitor. I will not sweep the floor every morning. You'll have to find someone else to do those things."

We had never heard anyone speak to our father so defiantly. We glanced at him to see if he was angry. Our astonishment increased when we saw by his trembling lips and smiling eyes that he was struggling to control his amusement.

"And furthermore," Miss Tucker went on in her high-pitched voice, "I will not live in that room you call a teacherage. I spent the last two nights there, and I won't spend one more. I will teach, but I need a decent place to live."

Miss Tucker had more to say, and my father listened politely. Evidently he saw an educator in this strong-minded woman from Arizona. He did find someone else to start the oil stove every morning, and it was arranged that Miss Tucker would live for half the school year with Mrs. Kennedy, the depot agent, and the other half of the year with the Houths, in their big house in the center of town. The teacherage remained empty that year.

Coming from teaching in a Phoenix school to teaching in Hunter School must have seemed to Miss Tucker like traveling a hundred years back in time. We children gloried in the relative spaciousness of our school compared to the cramped little houses most of us lived in. But to Miss Tucker, our school and our daily lives must have seemed the height of barbarism. She never grew accustomed to the wind tearing across the land, the complete absence of buses and taxis, and the loneliness of living in a little town with only seventeen inhabitants. Our relentless winter season, which left only a tiny margin on either side for a brief fall and a fleeting spring, was an abject hardship to her. She often spoke yearningly of Phoenix's warm climate.

We soon learned that Pearl Tucker landed in our remote part of the state entirely through her own miscalculation. When she saw the advertisement for the teaching position in our school, she must have assumed that all of Montana resembled the forested, snow-covered mountains of the western part of the state. Because of the erroneous visions she had entertained about her new teaching environment, she was very disappointed in the terrain of our Montana, a full five hundred miles east of picturesque Glacier National Park, the Rocky Mountains, and the Continental Divide.

But whatever Miss Tucker felt when she arrived in the prairie land of Montana's Hi-Line instead of the mountainous vistas of western Montana, she didn't let her feelings paralyze her. Instead she set about to prove that "Someday you will say I was the best teacher you ever had," a statement she made to us more than once.

Miss Tucker immediately demonstrated that discipline would not be a problem for her. She was definitely in charge of her classroom and we were all expected to learn. She had no patience with Marie Doyle's excuses for missing school; she gave Marie a blistering lecture for giving the dubious explanation that she had been absent the day before because of an ingrown toenail. Miss Tucker's sharp tongue made even the tough boys cry at least once. When Jerry Johnson met us in the morning with the warning, "Be careful, Miss Tuckah's on her high hoss!" we knew that we should tread softly that day.

My feisty sister Vivien bragged that she was the only student Miss Tucker didn't bring to tears during that year.

In the single classroom, students sat in rows in order of their grade, eighth-graders in the larger desks on the north side of the room near the door, and first-graders next to the bank of windows on the south side. While students in the remaining grades worked or read in their seats, the teacher called the students in each class to sit on the heavy black wooden bench behind her desk, where she drilled them. Sometimes the teacher assigned an older or more capable student to help a younger or struggling one. My older sisters often sat with Marie Doyle to help her with her long division.

Of the seventeen students in Hunter School, some— like us and Joe Morgan's grandchildren, the Bertelsons—lived on farms a mile or two from Hunter. The Doyles and the Houths lived close enough to walk to the school on Schoolhouse Hill every day, but all the students brought their lunches and ate together.

While we ate breakfast at home and my father braided my hair, our mother packed our lunches. They consisted of jelly sandwiches—or sometimes just butter with sugar sprinkled over the butter—and cookies, all packed in the gray metal lunchboxes we shared. Other students had more glamorous lunches, but poor Shirley Johnson, the only other student in my grade, had sardine sandwiches most days; we, unkindly, shunned the fishy smell where she sat at lunchtime.

Miss Tucker was all business during lesson time, but we saw another side of her during recess and the lunch period.

We ate lunch at our desks, with Miss Tucker sitting at hers in the front of the room and we in our wooden student desks, connected by wooden runners on the floor.

When our lunch was finished, sometimes Miss Tucker joined our games. During the cold winter months, we usually spent our playtime in the basement gymnasium playing basketball, pom pom pullaway, or roller-skating in strap-on metal skates. Miss Tucker brought us other games, such as "Mother, May I?" from her city classroom. When the weather was warm enough to play outside, we had just enough students in the school to have two teams for softball, and Miss Tucker was known to take her turn at bat, still wearing her shiny black high heels. She didn't run the bases. Someone else ran them for her.

A huge pile of dirt on the south side of the school, left from when the basement cavity had been dug years before, inspired another favorite activity. Now mostly grassed over, this five-by-eighty-foot mound of earth was home to dozens of gophers. We spent hours hauling buckets of water from the slough in the nearby wheat field to drown these poor animals out. Our city teacher did not participate in this savage recreation. When we heard the clang of the school bell from the bell room, we rushed back to Miss Tucker's flash cards, penmanship exercises, and grammar drills, and the gophers were safe for a time.

Despite her legendary ability to make her students cry and the fact that my brother called her "The Old Crab" for a time, Miss Tucker's year in our school was a rich experience for us. In her neat straight skirts and high heels, she brightened our lives and broadened our horizons.

We had never seen color photos before; she took

dozens of us all and gave them to our families. She gave us samples of candy and figs from Arizona. She told us about palm trees and dates and deserts. To us, her stories of Phoenix were like tales from *A Thousand and One Nights*. As a first-grader, I listened in while she taught the older students. When she recognized that I was reading beyond my grade level, she encouraged me. She let me write in script. We thrived under her tutelage. Through her intense teaching and rough affection, she made the outside world seem like a friendly, interesting place.

Miss Tucker returned to Phoenix after her year in northeastern Montana, and for a time she wrote to us regularly. In one letter, a year after she'd left northeastern Montana, she wrote, "I do so hope the children have a good teacher this coming year. . . Mrs. Wiedeman, had you ever thought of spending the winters down in Arizona and going back to put in the crops in the spring? Many farmers from Montana and North Dakota do that. I don't think Mr. Wiedeman would find it difficult to get something to do during the winter months, and I think the children would have better opportunities going through the Arizona schools. Of course, I may be prejudiced." In closing she wrote, "Please give all the children my love."

She often told us in her letters that she would like to see us again. She never once said she missed Hunter and Sheridan County. We Wiedeman children corresponded with her for years, and to this day, John Houth says she was the best teacher he ever had.

lou mandler

# Nine

# A Man Alone

One year, our father intervened in the discipline at Hunter School in a way that permanently fixed our image of him. Whispers and silences then and later, and one vivid scene, made this quiet man a hero to us. Whether we saw him truly or not, we afterwards held him prisoner as hero in our minds.

During the year of the trouble at school, Bruce was an oversized, bullying eighth-grader with a fleshy face and an eye for victims. At that time, my sister Agnes was a fifth-grader; Diana was in the first grade, Vivien was in the third with Marie Doyle, and my brother Arthur was in fourth grade.

I was a year too young for first grade and lived each day for the return of my siblings from school. Through their stories and talk, I created a mental picture of the classroom, adding characters and routines with the recital of each day's events.

By now, I knew that big Bruce was the largest and scariest student in the classroom. I had heard that he twisted the arms of the younger boys and threatened to beat them up. Although these boys tried to stay away from him, they couldn't always keep out of his menacing path in a one-room school. In the classroom of my young imagination, Bruce loomed large as a figure to be feared.

My father's involvement with the safety of Hunter's classroom began one day when Marie was sitting with us in our kitchen eating an after-school snack of my mother's spice cookies.

"That Bruce!" she began, as my mother sat listening to the chatter of school girls. I don't know exactly what Marie told my mother that day because Mama sent us little girls out to play, but it was enough to set things in motion. That night at supper, my mother asked, "At school, Mrs. Martini, does she try to make Bruce behave?"

"Oh, she can't," Vivien replied. "She's afraid of him."

Perhaps it was then that my brother chipped in to say, "He asks me things like, 'Have you ever seen your sisters naked?' and the teacher doesn't do anything."

I can see even now how my parents would have exchanged looks and tightened their expressions at these remarks, and I can feel the freighted silence which would have followed this table talk.

That day was the beginning of a time when something serious was in the air, something not to talk about with children. To any questions about it, Mama's breezy answer was, "Oh, never mind." Mama could keep a secret as well as she could tell a story. I know now that my parents discovered Bruce had committed unsavory acts beyond what was described in the conversation at our table.

When Daddy went to town that week, he included a visit to the county superintendent. Then he went to a school board meeting. As clerk of the board, he always went to board meetings, but the next morning we learned this had not been a routine meeting. My mother told us that Bruce would not be in school any longer. The board had expelled him.

To a voiced, "Why?" she offered only an enigmatic, closed-mouthed "Because."

It soon became clear that not everyone in the community or on the school board believed Bruce should have been expelled. A day or two later, Bruce's father and a small group of neighborhood men, led by postmaster and elevator owner Raymond Houth, arrived at our farm to speak with Daddy. My mother herded us into the house, where we crowded around the window to watch my father meet his neighbors in the yard.

I can still see the pantomime we watched through the window that day. Raymond Houth did much of the talking, gesturing with his hands. The other men stood beside and behind Raymond, watching my father intently. Finally I saw my father speak—perhaps a sentence. Raymond Houth responded, and now I could hear only the tone of his raised voice. I could see Daddy speak again but I heard nothing. He stood alone with his head lifted and his back straight, his hands in his pockets. Flanked by other serious-faced men, Raymond Houth—tall, forceful, and arguing—stood facing our determined father. Mama, standing behind us, observed the scene too, punctuating our silent watching with tense, audible breaths. Finally, our angry visitors drove away, and our huddle in front of the window broke apart in relief.

Bruce's father resigned from the school board in protest of the expulsion. Bruce never returned to school. Because the school was the only community gathering place left in Hunter, we hardly saw Bruce and we mostly didn't think of him. Perhaps because my mother was much more apt to talk about black sheep than about acorns falling close to the tree, our horror of Bruce's actions did not cause us to shun or scorn his family. We played with his brother, and after a time, my father did business with his parents.

However, in a few years, Bruce again interrupted the lessons in our school. By this time I was in the third grade. Our teacher that year, Mr. Jensen, lived in the teacherage with his wife and, incredibly, three children. He was listening to my first-grade sister Betsy read at the bench behind his desk. I was watching Betsy bob her head as each word struggled out when I heard a sharp crack from the teacherage. Soon the door opened, and Mrs. Jensen's white, frightened face appeared in the space of the partially opened door. Mr. Jensen immediately went to her, and they disappeared inside their one-room home.

When he emerged, he told us that we would not be allowed outside that day. Someone had fired a rifle through the window of the teacherage. We spent most of our lunch hour gazing at the lace-edged bullet hole in the window and wondering who had fired the shot. In the days that followed, we learned that Bruce had done it. I never knew or don't remember what happened to him for this. Or whether it was random or deliberate.

After I had been gone from home for some years, I heard the news that Bruce's life had come to a violent end. He had shot and killed a local man and died in return gunfire. There had been arguments and threats over broken promises and monies owed. In the final confrontation, Bruce erupted in rage and began shooting with the pistol he had brought to this final gathering. And so it happened that Bruce never got the money he thought was owed him. Instead he and one other lost their lives.

Today I puzzle over the anger that had so affected Bruce's life and, finally, ended it. His dismissal from Hunter School was just one instance of the pain and anguish his tormented life and sporadic violent acts inflicted on his own and other families. My mother wasn't alone in her tendency to discriminate a black sheep from a fallen acorn. Decades later, Helen Doyle said to me, "I felt so sorry for his mother when all those awful things with Bruce happened, and you know, he was good-hearted sometimes. It was just that he had a terrible temper."

It has been many years since Bruce was expelled from a little country school. At the time, silence surrounded the incident. Even fifty years afterward, a neighbor said to me, "Oh, it's better not to talk about that." Now I know that, with the support of the county superintendent, my father was responding to a situation of sexual molestation amongst school children. Then I only knew something shameful had happened and that my father seemed to have acted alone, earning a reputation in the community for being a stubborn man, a man not to tangle with. The silent scene I witnessed from our window did far more than any story to fix my childhood view of my father. I couldn't help but preserve the image of him facing the rest of the world in our yard: a man alone except for my mother, signaling her loyalty with each tense breath.

# This Storied Land

lou mandler

Part Two

# Seasons of Childhood

lou mandler

# Ten

# Ice in Summer

My sister Lillian was born in June after I completed the second grade. That summer would be even busier than most. On the little rise across the yard, south of our house, a new one-and-a-half story house was going up. Daddy had made two trips in our red '49 International truck to Kalispell earlier in the spring to buy lumber from our uncle, Hans Olmquist, who ran a small sawmill after he and my mother's sister Emily moved west. Because my father had to spend most days in the fields, he hired two carpenters from Plentywood, Herb and Marvin, to frame the house.

Herb and Marvin were partners in carpentry, but there

were no common traits in their appearance except for the white carpenter overalls they both wore. Silent Herb was sandy-haired, pale, thin. Marvin's belly pushed his overalls out in the front; he was short, dark-eyed, dark-skinned, and talkative. We children spent hours watching Herb and Marvin mark chalk lines and hammer nails. They ate with us at noon, giving my mother ten to cook for in addition to the new baby she nursed each day. We relished the novelty of having extras at our table, and we stared as Marvin washed in the metal wash bowl and then looked in the mirror to comb his bushy black eyebrows before he sat down to eat.

When the house was framed, Herb and Marvin moved on to another job, and when the harvest was done, my father worked on the house alone. Though the floors and woodwork were unfinished and the walls unpainted, we moved into the new house on New Year's Day, an unseasonably mild first day of the year. We didn't mind the roughness of our new house. We had glorious space. My brother had his own bedroom downstairs; we five older girls took the upstairs bedrooms, two in one room and three in the other. Our baby sister's crib, the same crib my father had welded together for his first-born, stood in the corner of our parents' bedroom.

By the next summer, the old house was temporarily abandoned. My father hadn't yet put it to other uses. In time, he jacked up the lean-to kitchen, put skids under it, and with the Farmall tractor pulled it across the yard where it become a garage for the new house. Using the same method, he moved the center section of the old house to a corner of the yard to serve as a small granary. In still another corner, the sturdy little entryway that my father had built became a support for fuel tanks. He demolished only my parents'

# This Storied Land

former sleeping space, the enclosed porch, which was too flimsy to transform to another use.

In that summer following my sister's birth and our move to the new house, the old house stood empty and unused, sheltering only boxes of old magazines: *Saturday Evening Post, Country Gentleman, The Farm Journal.* Most of these magazines included some fiction in each issue, usually short stories of pretty young women in high heels falling in love with dashing young men. One July day, I escaped to the old house and sat down on the worn linoleum floor, ready for a summer afternoon of reading. The smell of mice and the accumulated dust were only momentary drawbacks, and the waiting silence of the empty room was soon peopled with characters from my absorbing story. Real time was suspended as I was sucked into another time, another world.

Suddenly, darkness came to join the quiet in my reading room. Could it really be nightfall? I went outside. I looked to the west and there, behind the windmill, was the blackest cloud I had ever seen, filling the entire western sky. The air was still. I saw no one. The world was bathed in eerie day-night tones. A flutter of fear sent me running across the yard toward the new house. Once inside, I glanced at the clock on the wall. It was still afternoon—2:43 p.m.. My sisters stood around, their mouths stilled, and their eyes moving with fearful questioning. My mother, mouth pinched around her worry, was on her feet where she could see through both the north and west windows. She was watching sky and road, reading the storm signs above, and fretting about my brother and father, who were working in the fields.

Soon my brother drove in on the yellow Minneapolis Moline tractor and came running inside. Then my father arrived, driving the pickup from where he had left the red Farmall tractor in the field. We all gathered inside the house as the world turned even darker. Then the wind began, and almost immediately, rain. Loud rain.

"It's hailing!" my father said. "Get the windows!" Blankets and pillows materialized, some to each child.

"Hold them over the windows!"

We did our best, our arms stretched to the tops of the windows, our bodies holding blankets or pillows against the lower panes. But the wind sent new-potato sized hailstones pounding furiously against house and the windows. The glass could not withstand this barrage of stones of ice, and soon we were holding up the blankets not to keep the panes from breaking but to keep broken glass, rain, and hailstones out of the house.

"My window is gone!"

"Mine too!"

"Ouch, it hurts!"

"There's glass on the baby!"—this last from Betsy, who was watching not a window but our little sister.

When the storm was over, we children ran from window to window inspecting the dark results of Nature's icy barrage—the five broken windows, the drifts of white against the house, the dents in the cab of the truck in the yard. We dashed outside and collected hailstones, vying to find the largest. The hail had even shorn the leaves from the trees in the shelterbelt. This summer storm did not leave the treasured fresh smell of rain on dry soil; it brought the icy smell of winter.

I didn't pay attention to my father's tight face, my mother's scowl and jutting lip. My father drove out to the fields to inspect his crops. That night at supper, my mother and father held their usual places at the table's ends, but tonight they were both silent, and we were beginning to realize that this storm had been more than a freakish summer extravaganza. The next morning our mother confirmed our fears.

"The crops are gone," she said. "There's nothing left. The hail beat the wheat stalks right into the ground. It's going to be a tough year."

She went on to explain that the expenses of the new house made the losses of the storm even worse. And now there were the broken windows to replace.

"You kids aren't going to get much for school clothes this year," she said.

We learned that day, too, that the combination of hail and the deluge of rain had flooded the Little Muddy Creek in town. A woman and her teenage son had been killed when their basement wall collapsed on them. The sloughs were swollen with water, usually a richness to be savored. But this time the rains of heaven had brought destruction.

Winter's weight seemed to come to my parents early that year. Late August brought an unnatural quiet to the farm. The ice in summer had robbed my father of the usual harvest work with combine, truck, and grain auger. By now, I was well acquainted with qualities of silence. Some silences were fruitful, encouraging hopeful visions and pleasant feelings. This was an uncomfortable silence like the feeling at home on Sunday morning, when the fabric of the quiet was permeated with our guilty knowledge that it wasn't right that we weren't at meeting.

Even Leonard Norman's visits ceased for a time. With

no prospects for a crop, he had gone to Canada to spend the winter with relatives. Because there was no harvest, my father lingered over breakfast and we ate supper earlier than the after-dark suppertime of other August and September days.

After one of those early suppers, I settled in on our old leather couch, a cast-off from the Petersons, to enter the world of the woods of northern Michigan in *Girl of the Limberlost*. I fell asleep and awoke to the sun flooding the room and the smell of coffee and the rough music of breakfast dishes in the next room as my parents sat down to the meal they ate alone together. Bits of the farm stock market report from the radio floated in to me.

"Box beef yesterday thirty-five cents lower. 35.29 on those light weight choice kind of carcasses. . . The cash cattle in Texas and Kansas forty-four dollars and that's just about steady. . . Live cattle futures for August down twelve to 35.17. . ."

The radio was snapped off before the grain prices began.

"How many cattle do you think we have to sell to make it through the winter?" I heard my mother ask.

"Well, purt' near all the calves. We'll have to keep at least thirty cows to keep the herd going next summer."

"And then there's hay to buy, too," my mother said. The hail had robbed us of even that crop.

"Yeeah, it's going to be pretty rough."

There was a silence.

Then my father said, "I s'pose we could get something for him if we sold Rusty."

Three years earlier, Daddy had bought a red-brown horse, a companion for Snider and, my parents hoped, a horse for us to ride. But Rusty had a mean streak. He bit my sister's finger. He bucked my brother off. We soon left him alone. Now I was fully awake. I waited, wondering if my father would mention Snider. He didn't.

Then came the sound of a coffee mug being placed deliberately on the table and his words, "Oh, we'll get by somehow."

Later that fall, a man came and took Rusty away. Snider, my mother's very good friend, stayed.

lou mandler

# Eleven

# School in Town

The year I turned eight, our family began to enter a new era. First, we moved out of our crowded little homesteader's house into the new house. Then, the following year, we started attending school in Plentywood. It was an act that once again set my parents apart from the rest of the Hunter community.

In his role as clerk of the Hunter School Board, Daddy had always been in charge of finding a teacher for the school. It was a yearly, discouraging task. A professing woman who worked in the courthouse once told my mother that the courthouse workers knew when Daddy was visiting the county superintendent to discuss hiring a new teacher. Because he came so often, they had learned to identify the sound of his deliberate footsteps on the wooden stairs.

After Miss Tucker returned to Arizona, our teacher was a retired widow, Mrs. Bird, whose permed white hair and neatly dressed petite frame suggested the organization skills evident in her classroom direction. We giggled over her romantic liaison with a paunchy, city-suited businessman from North Dakota. I resented her for telling me I was too young to write in script; she made me print. I wrote, in script, to Miss Tucker to complain about this unfairness.

The following year, the Jensen family from North Dakota moved into the one-room teacherage. Devout Seventh Day Adventists, this engaging family gave us a sense of the world beyond Hunter and The Truth that, although not as exotic as Miss Tucker's Phoenix, was appealing. Slim Mrs. Jensen wore full, flared skirts, and she pin-curled her short dark hair to create a curly crown. Mr. Jensen was genial and humorous, not pre-occupied with work, weather, cattle, and machinery. Despite their being part of what we thought was an odd, and certainly wrong, religion, we liked them. The Jensens' young daughter was a friend of mine and my sister Diana's.

Kurt, their tall sixteen-year-old son, ruffled the calm surface of our family life in a new way. He and my seventh grade sister Vivien struck up a relationship. Even as a third grader, I was aware of how this adolescent affair of the heart alarmed my parents. Not only was there a five year age difference between Vivien and Kurt, but never before had one of us had a relationship with someone of the opposite sex. As it turned out, none of us ever would again while we were living at home. Gratification of the yearnings and stirrings of developing sexual appetites was delayed for us all until after we left home.

My parents didn't forbid Vivien from seeing her boyfriend. In the tagging of the different children in our family, my little sister Betsy was "Mama's girl" because she was a shy, clinging child, and Diana was the "stubborn" one. Deserved or not, spirited Vivien was the "troublemaker." As an adult, my brother commented, "Whenever I got into trouble as a kid, Vivien was always there." Perhaps my parents knew that forbidding contact between Vivien and Kurt Jensen would spark rebellion in Vivien. I don't know what they said to my sister, but that spring was the only time when the students from Hunter School, joined by Kurt, came out to our farm every day after school. My father let us set up a softball diamond on the alfalfa field below the house. There my sister and her friend saw each other daily as we all played softball outside the windows of the house where my mother worked and near the fields my father tended.

As all the teachers had before them, the Jensens, too, moved on the following year. Vivien and their son wrote letters back and forth for several years.

The summer before I was to begin the fourth grade, it was more difficult than ever to find a teacher for Hunter. Only Mrs. Martini was available, and our family knew how Mrs. Martini ran a classroom. It was she who did nothing to protect the little children from big Bruce a few years before. She said unkind, belittling things to her students. Nevertheless, with no other option, the Board reluctantly decided to hire her. My parents decided that Mrs. Martini would not teach us; they would scrape together tuition money and send us to school in town.

Because our local school was still open, we had to provide our own transportation to school in Plentywood. My mother didn't drive, and if my father drove us every day, he would lose more than two hours a day from his farm work. My fourteen year old brother Arthur had driven tractors, pickups, and trucks for years so it was decided that he would drive the six of us in our maroon Kaiser the fifteen miles to school. Since he didn't have a driver's license, Mama and Daddy instructed him to avoid the highway and drive the back way, on gravel and dirt roads past Joe Morgan's farm, through the coulees surrounding it. We sat three in the front seat of the Kaiser and three in the back. All that year we traveled a furtive route to school—back roads, back entrance to town, side-street parking place.

Changing from a one room school with sixteen students to a school that had two classrooms for each grade was tremendously exciting but also sad and scary. Although we were eager to meet new people and to know more about town people, we were also sure everyone was going to be smarter than us, that we would look shabby beside the town kids, and we were sad about leaving Hunter School. Our first fear soon proved to be unfounded; we could hold our own in the classroom. And having just two dresses to wear on alternate days didn't make us untouchables. We made friends, but we did think of Hunter School with nostalgia.

By the time we started attending Plentywood School, my father had mysteriously stopped taking us to regular Sunday morning meetings, and we occupied the cultural borderland being a part of neither The Truth nor the "world." A few children from The Truth attended school in

Plentywood, but we did not automatically form an alliance with them. We were not quite a part of their world although we were even more not a part of the dancing, movie-going, TV-watching, jewelry-wearing world. I yearned to belong to one of these worlds. The attraction of belonging to the small group of children from The Truth was the reward of being right, of living a divinely approved life, but I also felt a pull towards the freedom and glamour and creativity of the worldly children.

Weighing in and deciding the tug of war between these two forces was the simple but potent power of family. I existed smack in the middle of this family in which there was an unspoken understanding that it was unthinkable to venture beyond the clearly defined boundaries of our lives. It may not have been true, but it felt like testing the boundaries would jeopardize one's place in this most important group. I satisfied my taste for risk and variety in other ways—physical activity, and vicariously, through reading. It wasn't until I had been away from home for some time that I let myself question, investigate, look at other ways of living.

Since we were not free to choose, we somehow carved out a livable niche between these two worlds. It helped that we were good students. For some of us, for my sister Diana and me in particular, it helped that we were good at sports. Playing softball and running races on the spacious fields next to Hunter School and hauling hay during the summers had instilled in us a love of physical activity, and competing with older students had taught us to be scrappy.

At Plentywood School, I sometimes chose to play games with the boys during the long noon recess rather than join the more sedate play of the girls on the playground equipment. For a while, I joined a pick-up basketball game on the outdoor court. At that time, I was experimenting with a "grown-up" hairdo for my braids, arranging and pinning them on top of my head.

One day, wearing my new hairstyle and a hand-me-down dirndl-skirted grey dress with a black velvet collar, I was playing basketball with my fifth grade male classmates when Mr. Wollan, the superintendent, walked by on a tour of the playground. I was intent on stealing the ball from Jimmy Harrington when I heard Mr. Wollan yell, "OK, Mary Lou! Get that ball! All right! Come on now, Mary Lou!" I'm sure I remember that scene because even then I understood he didn't often see a tall fifth-grade girl in a dress, glasses and an old-fashioned hairdo fighting with a boy over a basketball.

As long as we were in grade school, Diana and I had an outlet for our love of physical competition. Each spring, all the schools in the county came to Plentywood for a Play Day during which the students competed in races. My sister and I loved Play Day and looked forward to it each year. The ribbons we won there earned us a reputation for being the kids to beat. Then we entered high school and competition for girls ceased. Boys could join the football or basketball teams. They could run track in the spring. Girls could only cheerlead. We bitterly resented being locked out of athletic competition.

Arthur took us in the Kaiser on our secretive back route to school for only a year. My parents' decision to keep us from Mrs. Martini's indifferent instruction proved to be the death knell for Hunter School. Without us, only twelve students remained in the school. When Mrs. Martini abruptly abandoned her position before the school year was over, a neighboring farm wife taught the students as best she could for the rest of the year. The following year, the school closed, and we were reunited with our former schoolmates when all sixteen Hunter children rode to school in Plentywood in a big yellow bus. The sturdy Hunter School was sold and moved to town where it became an implement shop before it burned to the ground in the 1970s.

With the Hunter School Board no longer meeting regularly, our father seemed less a community figure once we began school in Plentywood. I learned, however, that memories are long. One day, two of the high school boys, John Houth and Paul Johnson, were suspended from riding the bus for fighting. Just before they appeared before the Board to petition to regain their ridership, one of my sisters overheard John Houth say to Paul, "I'm worried. I'm afraid of old man Wiedeman." I was surprised. I had thought only Daddy's children remembered his lonely stands against community opinion. And I didn't think he was old.

lou mandler

# Twelve

# Casting Out

*. . . where you stand*
*Surrounded, detached, in measureless oceans*
*of space,*
*Ceaselessly musing, venturing, throwing, seeking*
*the spheres to connect them,*
*Till the bridge you will need be form'd . . .*

—Walt Whitman, *A Noiseless Patient Spider*

## lou mandler

Mostly, we Wiedemans lived alone, in a small family community sustained by each other, supported by our parents, challenged by but savoring weather and space. Since the Olsons were invisible, we had no close extended family, and no visiting friends besides Leonard Norman. On rare occasions my sisters, Betsy and Diana, or I invited a school friend to sleep overnight. Sometimes my parents cast out from our island to connect with family members who had gone elsewhere.

Two years after my father drove our red truck to Kalispell and filled it with lumber to build our new house, he drove it to Kalispell again, but this time he had transformed it into a modern, motorized conestoga. We were all going traveling to see my mother's sister Emily and her family.

My mother's only family converse was with her sister, and she had moved away. Early in my childhood, Emily and Hans had lived nearby and visited us often. They brought a sense of fun with them. Hans teased us and told jokes. Emily's regular giggle made you want to laugh with her, to see life as she did. My mother and her sister had long talks in the kitchen.

After Emily and Hans moved to western Montana, we knew them mostly through the letters that my mother and Emily wrote back and forth. My mother didn't always take time to sweep or mop her floor, but she wrote to Emily regularly.

It was the summer I turned ten that my father fashioned a camper on the back of the truck so we could visit Emily and Hans. First he welded an arching metal frame over the truck box and then stretched a gray-green tarp over the frame. Five of us children would ride in the space under the tarp while my parents and youngest sister would travel in the truck cab. En route we would pick up my sixteen-year-old sister Agnes from the farm just east of Glacier Park where she was working for a family in The Truth. We bought a pup tent for my father and brother to sleep in; my mother and her five daughters would sleep on the floor of the truck box and on some old car seats my father had placed inside the box.

As this trip was being planned, my sometimes contrary fourteen-year-old sister Vivien announced, "That's embarrassing, traveling in a truck, and I'm *not* going." Despite her adolescent distress about her family's public display, plans for the trip proceeded. My father made arrangements for one of the Morgans to do our chores—milking the cows, feeding the bull in the morning and evening. We cleaned the house so it would be presentable when Rowena Morgan used our kitchen to wash the cream separator after her husband was done with the milking.

Our excitement on the day we left was dampened because one of my father's eyes was red and painful. He had been welding and when he'd removed his protective hood to chip slag off a new weld, a piece of the metal hit him in the eye. Looking at his red watery eye made me grit my teeth against the obvious pain. "Oh, it'll be all right," he said, shrugging off my mother's concern.

As we began our journey in our dark conestoga and drove past the crossroads two miles south, I looked east. I could see the top of the grove of trees in the hollow where the Olsons lived, and I thought how strange it was that we were about to drive five hundred miles to see my mother's sister, but we never saw the rest of her family who lived fifteen minutes from us.

We didn't make many miles that first day. By the time we had reached Wolf Point, my father's eye was too painful for him to continue driving. We camped by the side of the road. Daddy had strapped the old bottled-gas stove into a corner of the truck, and Mama warmed a couple quart jars of home canned beef for our supper. Arthur doled out peanut butter and oatmeal cookies from the coffee cans my sister Diana had packed for our trip. Vivien, who of course had come after all, went to sleep early.

Daddy's eye was no better the next morning. My mother, no doubt thinking of her own father's lost vision, insisted we stop in Glasgow, where they found a doctor. After discerning a sliver of metal in my father's eye, the doctor carefully extracted it, and my father drove on, wearing sunglasses to shield his eye.

U.S. Highway 2 reaches across Montana's Hi-Line for more than four hundred level, sky-rimmed miles. We stopped in Dodson, Joplin, Havre. Then we drove on towards our first scent of pine forests, our first sight of a waterfall, our first view of a mountain, our eagerly anticipated visit with our aunt and uncle.

With high spirits, we loosened the tarp over the cab, tied it back, and stood with the wind rushing through our hair, watching the road ahead. The people in the cars speeding towards us stared, and we waved vigorously to all of them. Most of them waved back. Finally, my father stopped the truck to warn, "Hey, you kids better quit that!" We didn't understand at the time that when my father saw others staring above the truck cab he thought something might have gone amiss with his tarp creation. His self-effacing nature may also have been chagrined by our gregarious enthusiasm, for his standards of acceptable behavior did not include drawing attention to oneself.

Our mother must certainly have requested the last stop we would make before entering Glacier Park: the Museum of the Plains Indians in Browning. Once Mama had sized up someone or something and found goodness, she dug her heels in, set her jaw, and opened her heart forever. All Indians had long been safely inside her fierce affections. The quiet respect she showed for the dimly lit Blackfeet museum must be, I thought, the way people act in a church. I had never been inside a church, but the elkskin dresses and the panorama of the buffalo jump evoked spirits of the dead and thoughts of lost tribes. However, when we emerged into the dusty streets of Browning, the sight of an elderly Blackfeet man with his hair in old-style braids reminded us that his was a living, though struggling, culture.

When our wagon-like truck pulled into St. Mary's campground in Glacier Park, Vivien's premonitions of embarrassment proved true. "Hey! Look what the cat dragged in!" we heard someone yell from a nearby rig. At another stop, a child stared at us and said to his mother, "Are those people gypsies?"

We didn't always inspire jokes or questions in our tarp-covered camper. As we pulled into the scenic overlook on Logan Pass, and the six of us tumbled out from the back of the truck, a group of Indian tourists in saris and other traditional dress smiled and snapped pictures of us. Vivien found even this to be embarrassing, and she buried herself in a book about a young Swedish woman, Lillian Budd's *April Snow*. I read the book when she finished it, and I will always associate the icy glaciers of Glacier Park with the tale of

Sigrid, the Swedish heroine who gave birth in a snow tunnel.

Vivien did join us at a campfire talk where the park rangers taught us the Song of the States. For years afterward, as we hauled bales or whiled away time during an electrical outage, we would belt out, "Oh, what did Ida Hoe, boys, oh what did Ida Hoe?" And the response, "She hoed a merry land, boys, she hoed a merry land," and on through "what did Missis sip?" and "what did Della wear?"

Our days in the Park were an exotic change from our flatter world. We breathed in the rich aroma of pine trees, not the smell of dry prairie soil and grass; we saw deep mountain lakes, clear and brilliant blue, not the shallow, grass-filled sloughs of home, and the wind didn't blow here. My brother had walked miles and miles on the prairie, never fearing that he would get lost. In the Park one day, he headed up a trail to see a wonder called a waterfall. On his way back, he followed his curiosity away from the trail and suddenly understood that here he could lose his way. He was relieved when he came in sight of the campground.

The Going-to-the-Sun Highway in Glacier Park, with its mind-reeling, double-back turns and the abrupt, mile-deep drop on the edge of the road, capped our Park experience. We laughed as we looked into the cab at my frightened mother, sitting as close as possible to my father and refusing to look into the scenic pit below.

And then we were in Kalispell, at the Olmquists'. Visiting Emily and Hans was different from visiting Uncle Barney and Aunt Tillie in North Dakota. Because they didn't profess, our aunt and uncle on our mother's side had a tang of worldliness about them. Emily's hair was bobbed, she wore pants, Hans smoked, we thought he probably drank beer. All

# This Storied Land

this piqued our curiosity, but Emily's comfortable giggle and her easy way with food and children was like our mother's. In these qualities and in their eager visiting, we saw our mother as someone's sister; talking, laughing, listening.

*Emily had regularly written letters to our mother throughout the years. While clearing out one of Mama's dresser drawers at the end of her life, I discovered a batch of letters from Emily to my mother which partially explained why their sisterly bond seemed especially firm. Besides being sisters, theirs was a bond of shared pain, of experiencing living as their mother's daughters. On page after page and in letter after letter, Emily poured out the trials of living near Grandma Olson in her last years. Her words built an image of a very difficult woman indeed.*

*After a visit from relatives, she wrote, "Course Grandma squeals and hollers around as only she can and no one else can visit."*

*After a funeral, Emily described her mother's actions, "I asked Mrs. S why she was so mad at me and its cause of the flowers and I wasn't to make any of the arrangements cause I wasn't a Lutheran. . . Oh! Well—if she's judge of mankind I'm doomed. . . We tried, but you know I never felt welcome in their house."*

*"She has so much hate and fight in her," Emily wrote more than a year later. "She sure is a worry. I'm afraid to go down really and I'd never go there alone."*

*Mixed in with descriptions of trying days were flashes of sharp humor quite like my mother's, "She says all her kids hate her—I told Mrs. S she ain't so dumb." I could almost hear Emily's wicked giggle. But then she would express the need to pull back, to disengage, "P.S. I get so mad at myself when I get to writing about her."*

We saw our father relax with Hans, showing us a completely new side of him. To see him visiting comfortably with a friend was a rare experience. We ate meals outside. We tasted maple-nut ice cream. We went home.

Six years later we broke out of our tight family community again when we boarded the Empire Builder to Washington State to visit my father's family. My mother's intense respect for our Wiedeman grandparents and the letters Grandma Wiedeman wrote regularly had already established our father's parents as the moral standard for our own family.

I was fifteen when we took the train to Washington, and I still had never set foot on the Olson farm four miles south of ours, where my mother's parents and her brother and his family lived. The people with whom my parents did share a spiritual kinship had abandoned this part of Montana, moved away to places where life is kinder. To maintain precious familial ties, my parents wrote letters and made pilgrimages.

Years later, one afternoon in Connecticut, I stood on the top of the hill where we live, above the village green. The world was March-drab, and spring's promise was not yet evident. Then the haunting cry of geese drifted from the sky. I looked up. This was a sight and sound that had made me, as a child, think of the world beyond. It was a sound of seeking, yearning, travel, a chorus of calling, responding. This *V* shape was the sight of a family pattern, moving through space and time, changing places in formation, traveling from one home to another, guided by an unerring sense for each destination. I wondered if my parents heard the geese in the fall and the spring and thought, as I did, of the ones who had left home and come back for a time, only to leave again. Of those who don't come back. Of those who are left alone.

lou mandler

# Thirteen

# Liver for Supper

The sun dominated most of the summer days of my prairie childhood. In summer, the yellow sun in the blue bowl of sky looked for us, found us, and kept us in its hot line of power. I thought the sun must like this prairie land where there are so few pockets or wrinkles to hide in and where the dry earth doesn't sustain trees to shade vulnerable white-skinned humans. In fact, the sun's stare seemed to cleanse the world.

The sun's position in the sky told my father the time within the quarter hour. But more than a teller of time, this sun dried the hay quickly and scorched us as we stacked the prickly bales from the field and hauled them in. It burned our necks and arms as we knelt between the potato plants in the garden, plucking the black and orange potato bugs from the leaves and dumping them into cans of gasoline. When my father climbed onto his yellow tractor to go to the fields to summerfallow, mow, or pick rocks, he wore a visored cap, gray and blue striped, to soften the sun's glare.

One day I hadn't heard Daddy start the tractor and we weren't hauling bales. I cast about for something interesting to do. The house was quiet and cool, a victory for my mother in her daily summer battle against the heat of the sun. By ten o'clock each morning she had closed and curtained the windows to retain the coolness of night, defiantly securing her house from the invasion of the day's hot air. This day, the noon meal finished, we seven children had scattered.

My three older sisters were discussing clothes and looking at mail-order catalogs in their room. My brother had disappeared. Mama always seized the baby's nap as an opportunity to read another few pages in her current book. I was restless. I wanted action.

"Where's Daddy?" I asked my mother.

"He's butchering today. And you stay away from there."

Unlike the fathers of my friends at school, my father shielded his children from anything he thought might upset them. We didn't watch the cows giving birth, and we were banned from the barn when the young bulls were castrated. He didn't offer words to explain our banishment from such rites, and, although we wondered whether our mostly silent, hard-working father just didn't want us in the way, we knew it had more to do with his sense of rightness.

# This Storied Land

Because Daddy preferred action to speech, we watched him carefully to know his feelings and reactions. We knew he fixed his own machinery and even invented machines or gadgets to do particular tasks on the farm. He picked the first spring crocuses and brought them to the house. He never raised his voice and had stopped spanking his children because, according to Mama, it bothered him. My mother didn't drive so he bought the groceries in town. He never wore soiled field clothes to town but always changed into clean overalls and shirt. Picking up on Mama's example, we all felt oddly protective of Daddy, aware of what seemed a core discomfort or sadness in him. A mild rebuke from him mortified us. In the rare moments when my mother complained about one of his occasional missteps, such as forgetting to pick up ten pounds of flour in town, we instantly leapt to his defense.

Twice a year he butchered a steer behind the closed doors of the big shed, and my mother did her part in keeping us away. Life was hard enough, they thought, without children being involved in butchering. All we knew of the business of butchering was seeing Daddy bring the liver, heart, and tongue in a pan of salt water to the house. Supper on butchering night was always fried liver.

When I wandered outside on this summer butchering day, I had thoughts of riding the bike or looking for my brother, who might be catching frogs in the slough. He had read that expensive restaurants served frog legs as a delicacy, and he had decided to sample this food of the rich. Our brother's curiosity had, the winter before, inspired him to skin and fry a muskrat in my mother's iron skillet. The thought of dining on frogs and muskrats made me shudder. Arthur could catch frogs alone, I decided.

The hardened clay yard that stretched within the circle of our house, shed, and barn baked in the sun. Only insects produced the sounds and movement of that afternoon; flies, dragonflies, and grasshoppers buzzed and whirred their pleasure at the warmth of the sun. This was no day to ride a hot metal bike.

I stared at the doors of the white shed where Daddy butchered. Inside it would be dark and cooler. Daddy didn't usually butcher in the summer. He usually did it in the fall or spring when we were in school. I found myself walking towards the shed. When I stood before the white doors, I glanced back at the house. If anyone—my mother or my sisters—saw me spying on Daddy, I would be in deep trouble. I saw no one.

I stepped up to the door and fit my eye to a crack through which I could see inside. In the dim interior, I saw my father's back in the center of the shed. The familiar faded blue of his work shirt was the only color that showed against the weathered wooden walls and darker dirt floor. He was standing next to the black Angus steer that had lived in the pen next to the barnyard for the past few months. We had filled afternoons of boredom by bringing this stout animal handfuls of grass, which he reached for with his long tongue. We had taken turns brushing the hay-dust and dirt from his back.

Now, my eyes searched the shed's murky interior, and I could make out the halter around the steer's head and the dull gold of straw spread around his hooves. I had seen a picture something like this before—my father working with his cattle, sometimes to lead them to new pasture, sometimes to coax them to shelter. But today he was holding a gun.

In the next thirty seconds, the gun cracked and transformed the still tableau of Daddy and our steer. I saw the steer slump to the ground, his legs giving way, in a grotesque collapse. I heard his grunts—"aauugh. . .aauugh. Aauugh,"— the slow explosive sounds of the last moments of life.

My father stood waiting for death with one hand on the gun, the other tucked into his overall pocket. His back was still. The steer now lay at his feet. My father's back blocked the sight of death, but it could not mute the sound of death. I heard one final choked breath, then silence. In horror, I turned and ran, my hands over my ears, my brain holding the strange sight of my father's waiting back in its familiar blue and gray clothing.

Late that day in the kitchen I watched as my mother lifted a glistening purple-red liver out of a white metal pan and onto the cutting board. Experienced in the way of uncooked meat, she and her knife didn't mind the blood the liver gave up as it became a dozen thin slices. She tossed each brilliant piece into a plate of flour before throwing the white-coated slices into black cast-iron frying pans on the stove. For the second time that day, I fled from my parent, away from the bright and bloody supper preparations.

I didn't eat my share of liver that night. I watched my father quietly eat his supper as usual while his seven children argued and chattered around him. He gave his food his full attention. For him, a meal was not a social event; it was a time to eat. My eyes fixed on his broad strong hands as they performed the tasks with knife and fork necessary to satisfy his hunger. I had seen his hands carefully cradle my little sister; they had braided my hair; they fixed things.

But today . . .

The next morning I opened the freezer to get a can of orange juice for breakfast. In the compartment next to the juice a few white wrapped packages from the last butchering remained. They were labeled in thick black ink in my father's bold and awkward hand: "Sirloin Steak," "Hamburger," "Stew Meat," "T-bone Steak." This was nothing new. We always had meat in our freezer. But today when I saw the white packages, I heard a labored grunting and I saw my father's impassive back. His hands.

I hastily closed the freezer door and hurried outside into the light of morning. The sun shone as it had the day before. I kicked at a rock, uncovering a crowd of beetles that scurried for a new dark hiding place. The sunbaked yard looked as it had except the white doors to the shed were open. Today the sun reached even into that dark place, but another image stayed in my mind.

# This Storied Land

lou mandler

# Fourteen

# White-Out

When I was very young I thought of snow as a reason for exhilaration. The winter I was six, a three-day snow buried the two miles of gravel road to Hunter School. We knew the county plows wouldn't make the fifteen miles out from Plentywood to the Hunter road and our farm for days. We wouldn't walk to school nor would Daddy be able to take us in the pickup. Instead, when the sun came out, Daddy harnessed Snider and Rusty, hitched them up to the old bobsled, and we piled on for an open-air ride to school. On the way, we pushed one another off the sled onto the snow and raced laughing to tumble back onto it. The snow seemed to have smothered all the normal farm sounds. No motors throbbed. The snow's authority silenced even the chirp of winter sparrow and the moan of hungry cattle. We heard only the whoosh of the sled runners, the snorting of Snider and Rusty and our own shrieks and calls as bobsled and horses bore us through this fantastic white world.

Miss Tucker, our teacher, read aloud to all sixteen school children for fifteen minutes each morning. The week after the big snow had given us the gift of the sleigh ride, Miss Tucker read us a newspaper account of a dead body found in the snow. The man had frozen to death during the recent storm. I pondered that strange situation. As far as I knew, the word "body" referred only to a person's torso. So was this really all that was left of the man in the snow? If so, what had happened to his head, arms, and legs? Did they automatically disappear when a person died? Or was it the job of the person who found a dead person to hack them off?

I knew about animal death. My father killed our cattle so we could eat the meat. But human death was new territory to me. Not long before, my sister Vivien had said to me, "Of course you're going to die someday, silly. Everyone dies. Do you think you're going to live forever?"

I had no answer. I crept into the crowded little bedroom we five girls shared, crouched on my sister Agnes's bottom bunk-bed, faced the wall, held up my hands, and stared at them. So these hands would someday be attached to a dead person. They wouldn't have blood flowing through them. They would be buried in the ground. At this time, The Truth's emphasis on salvation was not yet part of my life view, and thoughts of heaven or hell did not enter into this first realization of death. Intent, sober, staring at the hands and then at the pale green plaster-board wall, I thought for a good while. It wasn't fair. I liked living. I wouldn't always be with my sisters and Daddy and Mama, then. My hands and the shabby green wall receded. Vivien was right. I would die someday.

And now Miss Tucker's newspaper story linked human death and snow, the same snow that transformed our plain prairie world into a magical landscape. Without television and radio, we sought variety, fantasy and theater from nature. And nature gave us these in all seasons, especially in the winter. When the snow and wind worked together to form extraordinary, sculpted drifts several feet high, this natural magic was as inspiring as any human spectacle I could imagine. Jack Frost was as real to me as the Sandman and realer than Santa Claus. Surely only a supernatural being could bestow such delicate, elaborate beauty on the window-panes, the few trees, and the windmill. But now it seemed that Jack Frost had thrown a man down dead in the snow.

So, snow meant more than something to be joyfully welcomed. My mother certainly knew that snow and cold brought both beauty and horror; playground and tomb; invitation and menace. We often came into the kitchen on a winter morning to her excited announcement, "Well kids, it's thirty below this morning!" The defiance in her voice carried a victorious conviction that she could keep her children safe in the midst of such threatening cold. This was a challenge that —"So there, Jack Frost"—she could meet. When the snow came down heavily, her exulting "Whee! Look at it snow!" suggested a purer pleasure. Snow meant change and beauty, but it also meant much-needed moisture for the field soil to soak up in the March thaw. A winter without snow meant a drier summer and poorer crops.

Mama also understood Jack Frost's other, dangerous face. We children grew in a climate of admonitions about winter and precautions against its menace. The open land of the northern plains gives the wind hundreds of miles to work up an overwhelming strength and fury. When the wind, the snow, and the cold unite their energies, anyone foolish or unlucky enough to be caught in the resulting blizzard courts death. In the winter, my parents kept a shovel in the trunk of the car and blankets in the back seat. They stored extra water and food in the house.

My mother's confidence in outwitting winter did not extend to trusting that her children would be safe on the school bus that took us into Plentywood for school beginning in my fourth grade year. Rather, her imagination created specters of a bus stalled in a snowstorm overnight with six of her children inside. She did what she could to forestall such a catastrophe. She wouldn't allow any of us to go off to school without overshoes, a hat, or mittens. Affected by the "town" priority of looks over warmth, we left our ugly overshoes on the bus instead of wearing them to school. We rationalized that we would have them if the bus were caught in a snowstorm. Mama fussed because the bus heater depended on a running engine, and she nagged the school district to outfit it with a heater that would run if the engine stalled or ran out of gas. We pooh-poohed all this concern.

One winter day when I was ten, we ended a routine day in school and headed for the school bus. Clarence, our quiet driver, said nothing about the snow that was beginning to blow about as we clambered onto the bus for the trip home. As the bus climbed the hill east of town, the snow thickened and the wind intensified. Five miles out of town, we were in a white-out. Out of the side windows of the bus we could see only solid white—no flakes, no light, no sight of sky. The world outside the windows had just vanished, and instead of miles of plains, we saw only a white mass. Our sense of direction disappeared so that we couldn't tell north from south, up from down. We were almost dizzy. This snow tantrum, this wind tirade seemed alive. It screamed at us, threatened us, stilled our chatter. God and Jack Frost became one, and their combined angry energy seemed directed solely at our yellow school bus.

Inside the bus, I watched the quiet concentration of the older people—Clarence, our bus driver, and Olaf Johnson and my sister Agnes, who were in high school. Lacing my fingers together, I concentrated on keeping my bubble of terror from becoming a balloon. Nature's display of evil power reminded me of Miss Tucker's dead man in the snow, but that couldn't happen to me. I was only ten. Surely we would soon see the ordinary world again.

The bus crept along. Nobody talked. Clarence asked Olaf to walk in front of the bus to mark the edge of the road for him. We watched Clarence's back and tried to see Olaf's dark figure outside in the whiteness. Occasionally, Olaf came inside to warm up and to have a low-voiced talk with Clarence. The furred earmuffs on Olaf's cap were pulled down and the part of his face that we could see had turned scarlet from the force of the wind and icy snow. Snow caked his cap. Shirley Johnson in the front seat heard Clarence ask him, "Do you know where we are?"

"We're lost!" Shirley whispered to Dale Rosgard behind her, and a hissed "We're lost!" rolled from seat to seat.

I clasped my hands tighter, closed my eyes, and leaned against my sister.

The next whispered message from the front of the bus was "We're looking for Ole Barnes's farm!" Yes, the Barnes' Polled Hereford farm should be near, but would Jack Frost and God let us find it? Would we run off the road first? Would the bus stall, the heater stop, and would we all freeze to death? Olaf's new task was to find the Barnes' Polled Hereford sign that stood at the corner of their driveway. As we inched along, we could do nothing inside but watch, wait, and try not to cry. Some of the little kids were crying. Oddly, the back of Clarence's neck looked as it looked every day.

It was night by now. Suddenly, miraculously, Olaf found the sign. As we made our slow way into the Barnes' yard, the shelter from their trees and buildings cut the power of the wind. The world was partially visible. Inside the bus, we were changed. We could move; we were not sitting so straight now; we unclasped our knit fingers. John Houth started joking. Dale Rosgard stopped crying.

My bubble of fear became a bubble of excitement. All sixteen of us would have to stay overnight at the Barnes'! What fun! Mrs. Barnes' matter-of-fact welcome was comforting. She fed us stew for supper and pancakes for breakfast. Girls slept in beds; boys and Clarence slept on the living room floor. She put the little kids who wanted their mothers near her. I was having too much fun to think much about my parents.

By the next morning, the snow had displayed its decorator skills, sculpting itself into glacier-like shapes and throwing itself over the fields to attract the sun's rays. Tossed between sun and snow, the bright light made our eyes water. It was hard to remember yesterday's angry snow. The snowplow

# This Storied Land

had cleared the highway early, and the bus took us back to school. Some of the older girls were embarrassed because they had to wear the same clothes to school two days in a row. At recess, I told my teacher about our exciting night. I still didn't think of my parents.

When we trooped into our house from the bus that evening, Mama and Daddy were at their usual table places, my mother's daily baking ready to feed the hungry. Their eyes checked us one by one. Then Mama pumped us for our story. Our tale told, one of us asked, "So what did you do last night?"

My mother shook her head and grimaced. "Oh! It was terrible," she said. "We had no way of knowing whether you were stuck in the blizzard or safe in town. We were hoping you would stay in town." Nemont Telephone had not yet come to Northeastern Montana, and none of the farm families had telephones. As part of her emergency planning at the beginning of the year, my mother had made arrangements for us to stay with Joe Morgan's daughter in town should the roads ever be blocked. But were we at Bess Morgan's?

We owned a radio by then, and Mama and Daddy religiously listened to the weather forecasts. "We knew a blizzard was coming," Mama said.

By 4:30 p.m., the time our bus usually delivered us at the end of the driveway, the blizzard was already swirling around the house. My father, in his chair at the end of the table, usually had a view of the road to the south. That day the road wasn't visible. Neither Mama nor Daddy spoke of the dark possibilities they imagined.

"Daddy paced the house half the night," my mother said. It wasn't hard for me to visualize my father, hands thrust in his overall pockets, walking from window to window, his step light and careful in his work boots, trying to see into the swirling snow, hoping for a change. As the evening wore on, he wouldn't expect to see lights from the yellow bus emerging from the snow.

"There wasn't much we could do," Mama said the next day. "You can't stop the wind from blowing, you know." Darkness strengthened fear and stoked the imagination. Mama had taken Lillian, the only child still at home, to bed with her. "But I had awful dreams," she said.

Daddy didn't go to bed. He stayed beside the radio, switching from station to station, thinking that if we were staying in town, someone might try to send a message by radio.

When morning came the plows came through, and my father drove to town. He went straight to the superintendent's office to ask about the students who rode the Hunter bus. It was enough for him to hear we were in school. He drove home to tell my mother.

Years later, when I moved to New England, the fluffiness of its snow seemed to create only winter wonderlands. In New England, the snow doesn't blow as it does on the northern plains, where it sometimes seems to come, not from the heavens, but from the Arctic, sent by a gigantic wind machine. Here in Connecticut there are no hard crusts, few icy blasts, no blowing drifts. Rather, the snow falls straight down and piles evenly on the earth, trees, roofs. This moist snow is better for sliding, snowballs, and snowmen. The weather is hardly ever cold enough that the snow squeaks under your boots. Perhaps here delight in snow could crowd out fear?

# This Storied Land

In 1978, New England had a big snow. My husband, my three children and I enjoyed the novelty, the quiet, and the slowed pace that such a really big snow here brings. We burned wood in our fireplace, not the North Dakota lignite of my childhood. The schools closed. The children rolled and played in the snow. But soon the news told of a young boy in Massachusetts, just older than my son, who had disappeared during the storm. About six weeks later he was found—buried in a fluffy snow bank by the front door of his house. Not long after, an adult resident of the State Training School near us wandered out of her dormitory during the night. The door locked behind her, and she froze to death. I seemed to hear her cries in my sleep.

I have watched my children slide down the big hill near our apartment. Their joyful pleasure evoked those days of delight when we tumbled off the sleigh on the snow-covered gravel road. But sometimes on winter nights, when the wind does blow in New England, its sound cuts into my sleep and I struggle from dreams of children locked outside, or of a white, whirling chaos beyond the windows. The sound of the shrieking night wind becomes the voices of other children, young women, old men crying, pleading to come in from the cold. And I remember staring at my hands against a green plasterboard wall, and I know again human frailty, human strength, a mother's and father's fear for their children, and the beauty and terror of winter.

lou mandler

# Fifteen

# The Sparrow War

Diana was wearing a blue dress when she broke her arm. We were playing softball at Hunter School. She hit a grounder just short of second base, and she reached first just as my brother at first base caught John Houth's throw. They both went down, and the dust plumed above them. As she rolled over in the dirt, Diana and her blue dress became a blue blur. Regaining her footing immediately, she held out her right arm, displaying the funny bump in it. From behind home plate where I watched, envy vied with sisterly concern and tightened my throat. No one in our family had broken a bone before, and once again, my older sister was running ahead of me into life.

My tough sister Diana was two years older than I, and, it seemed, ahead of me in everything else too. Truly strong of hand and fleet of foot, she could throw a ball farther than I could, run faster, and hit better. When John Houth and the other boys at school tried to show her how well they played, she simply beat them and ran away. What she couldn't do through natural talent, she accomplished through determination. Once when she was a first-grader, the Hunter teacher, Mrs. Martini, asked her to begin singing the round *Row, Row, Row Your Boat* for the other sixteen pupils. She refused. Exasperated, Mrs. Martini asked, "Where do you get your stubbornness? From your mother or your father?"

"Both of them," she responded. It was this double dose of stubbornness that I tried to mimic when I needed courage. I followed Diana in everything, even into the Sparrow War.

The dry grasslands surrounding our farm supported birds of many kinds. In the summer, we awoke to the trill of the meadowlark which we had decided sounded like, "San Diego is a pretty place." The yellow-bellied flycatchers and kingbirds nested in our shelterbelt, and the barn swallows built their mud nests in the eaves of the granaries. We appreciated these birds for their grace and appetite for insects. Although we children also admired the red-winged blackbirds and their song of "ok-a-lee," the farmers found them bothersome. We thrilled to the occasional glimpse of a great horned owl with its magnificent wing sweep. But of all the birds that made their home on and around our farm, we most scorned the English, or house, sparrows. They far outnumbered the "good" birds and competed with the barn swallows for territory. The farmers saw the swallows as an insect-eating alliance, but they regarded the sparrows, far messier than the swallows, as a threat to their livelihood. The song of the sparrow was a song they would rather not hear. The fall of a sparrow was fine.

One year in the mid-'50s, the county agent's office, always interested in protecting the wheat crops, came up with a plan to reduce the number of English sparrows. The office advertised a contest, open to all county teenagers and aimed at curtailing this feathered nuisance. Whoever brought in the most sparrow legs and eggs would win first prize of fifty dollars, enough to buy a new bicycle. Arthur and Diana were excited by the idea of a contest and immediately began planning.

"How do we kill the sparrows? Shoot them?"

"But Daddy doesn't let us use guns."

"Besides, we wouldn't be good shots."

"And where can we find sparrow nests?"

They consulted my father.

"There are all kinds of sparrows in the stock shed. And you're welcome to the pesky things," he said.

The rectangular stock shed was a simple, inexpensive structure, large enough for thirty head of cattle. In the winter, it protected our livestock from the bitter weather. The walls were boards placed perpendicular to the barnyard floor, and bales of hay arranged on a wire lattice served as the roof. With this roof design, my father unwittingly provided homes for dozens of English sparrows, which made their nests in and between the bales.

Throughout the winter, cow manure accumulated on the floor of the shed to a depth of more than two feet, but the cattle walked over their own frozen excrement with no trouble. By early spring, the brown layers began to soften, and during the March thaw the odor of the warming cow dung from the barnyard signaled the coming of the new season. When spring had truly arrived, my father would remove a section of the shed's board wall, put the scoop on the red Farmall tractor, and transfer load after load of stinking brown goo to the back barnyard. But we couldn't wait for the shed to be cleaned before we started our bird war. Our friends at school had already begun collecting sparrow eggs and legs. There remained the question of how to capture the sparrows.

Arthur and Diana put their heads together.

"Maybe we can just listen for the cheeping of a sparrow, find the nest, and grab the bird out of the nest," said Diana.

Arthur was more experienced in the ways of wild things. He had trapped muskrats and spent hours observing the birds in the shelterbelt. "Naw. That won't work," he said. "They'll fly away. We need to stun them somehow. Then when they're lying on the ground, we can get them."

"I know! One of us can poke a stick into the bales and then when the sparrow flies out, we can swat it with a broom or a shovel or something."

"But what about the manure?" I finally chimed in.

"We'll have to wear boots, of course," Diana sniffed.

My queasy stomach prompted another question. "And how are you going to kill the bird after it's stunned?"

Both Diana and I looked at Arthur. "Well, I guess we'll just have to twist off its head," he said matter-of-factly. "They're so small, it won't take much."

I heard a sharp intake of breath. It could have been

mine. It could have been Diana's. I looked at my sister. Her lips had almost disappeared and her eyes narrowed as she thought about this proposal. I could see she was determined to prove her status as the toughest of the farm kids. All of us scorned the "town kids" who shrieked at spiders and went "eeuuu" over a spot of manure.

"Okay. Let's go," she said after a moment.

"No, not now. We have to wait till night when the sparrows are in their nests. During the daytime they're out flying around."

And so it was agreed that the Sparrow War would begin that night at dusk. We gathered sturdy brooms and high rubber boots. Beside them, Diana placed a wooden box lined with old newspaper.

"What's that for?" I asked.

"For the eggs and sparrows, dummy," she replied.

At nine o'clock Arthur decided it was dark enough to launch our attack. Armed with the brooms, we marched through the muted sounds that mark the margins of spring nights. The croak of an early-arriving bittern punctured the gathering darkness from the south slough, and we heard an owl's low hoot. A new mother cow called hoarsely for her calf in the pasture to the north. The unmistakable "pop pop pop" of a John Deere tractor sounded in a neighbor's field. A white moon hung above the east horizon, waiting for the sun's gold. It was an unlikely environment for war. Wars are like that.

In the center of the dark stock shed, one bare electric bulb hanging from a cord made a circle of light. As we entered, the manure tugged at our feet and swallowed them to above the ankles, forcing us to wrench a foot away from its grip with each step. I nearly lost my balance as I clumsily clumped my way inside, and cried "Help!", waving my arms desperately to avoid a face-forward plunge into the ooze. Diana giggled.

"Watch out!" she said, and feinted a push to send me backwards. For a moment we forgot our mission of death and shrieked into the closed space as we lurched after one another in slow-motion tag. But soon Diana said, "O.K., let's get some sparrows," and we stood at attention, our rubber boots half buried in manure.

Arthur gave strategic orders: "Diana, you stand over there. Remember, we'll have to be fast with our hands because we can't run in this gunk."

To me, he said, "Your job is to push the broom handle up into the hay. When a sparrow flies out, one of us will hit it with the broom and knock it down. Then we'll grab it, twist its head off, and we'll get the eggs out of the nest. Then when you know how to do this, we'll trade places. Ready?"

"Ready!" Diana said.

I nodded.

I lifted the broom and made a random poke up into the hay roof over my head. Nothing flew out, but a cheep came from within the bale. "You have to push harder!" my brother said.

My next thrust went further into the roof and I flinched at the flutter of wings as an alarmed sparrow flew frantically for escape. Arthur lunged toward it, but the flailing of his broom hit nothing. "Aaww! Again!"

Less tentative now, I pushed in a new spot and routed another startled sparrow from her home. This time Diana reacted in tune with the movements of the bird, and with a sharp sweep of the broom she knocked it down. It fell a few feet out of Arthur's reach, its crumpled light brown body scumbled against the darker surface. The viscous manure made a guttural sucking sound as, throwing the broom aside, Arthur stepped close enough to snatch up the sparrow in his bare hands. Diana and I watched, hypnotized, as he grasped the little brown bird's head in one hand, its body in the other, and with a quick twist of his wrists, parted the head from the body.

"You have to twist fast and hard," he said, "Or else it's too awful." He tossed the fluff of feathers into the box Diana had brought.

I swallowed and wrapped my arms around my upper body. I could feel my heart beating. Diana didn't seem to flinch. Thinking only of the hunt, she took her stance again, her legs held slightly apart for balance, broom ready, her mouth set and her eyes intent. I wanted to rush out into the peaceful dark, but I knew I had to stay at my post and do my part. Grimly, I took up my broom again. If I had to hit and kill, I'd show them I could be good at it.

I roused two more birds. They escaped. Then my broom sent one Diana's way. With speed and determination, she plucked the sparrow up and I saw the decisive turn of both her wrists.

"It's like wringing out wet clothes," she said.

Soon I had to prove my mettle. Arthur knocked a bird onto the manure within three feet of me, out of his or Diana's reach. I steeled myself to act. I could do this. They were watching. I picked up the seemingly weightless sparrow. It was warm and soft. I closed my eyes while I turned my wrists as swiftly and as sharply as I could. Then I looked down. Done! I threw the little body toward the box. But the warmth of the feathers and the twist of my wrists stayed with me.

Our sparrow harvest continued, punctuated by cries of "Got one!" and an occasional "Yikes!" as one of us avoided a forward pitch into the muck. Then it became routine: the tiny dull "thunk" of a feathered carcass hitting the newspaper in our wooden box.

After what seemed a very long time, my neck began to hurt from craning my head back and my arms ached from holding the broom aloft. I yearned to breathe clean air. The garish light of the naked bulb hanging from the ceiling silhouetted my brother and sister in a way that made them look like story figures. Strange figures. And the birds, now a small pile in our box, were really dead. The word "contest" had sounded like so much fun.

A welcome voice at the door broke into our grim game. "You guys! Mama says you have to come into the house."

Diana answered our little sister. "Yeah, we're coming. We have to count our birds first."

Diana bent over the box, counting as she moved each tiny bundle of feathers from one pile to another. Then she stood and announced, "We have fifteen." Her body no longer seemed the body of fire and steel that had fought the war against the sparrows. Her slim shoulders slumped a little as her eyes contemplated the mound of lifeless creatures. Then she turned and led us back to the house.

The night was blacker now than it had been before our war, but the moon shone enough to light our way. The bittern and the owl were silent.

The next day when my father drove to town, Diana went along to take what remained of our sparrow corpses to the county agent. The wooden box already smelled of death and was beginning to attract flies. When she returned, she said, "Well, someone has already brought in thirty-five and the Anderson boys have brought in twenty-eight. There's no point in going to the stock shed again tonight." I heard relief in her voice, and our eyes met in understanding.

That afternoon we resumed our normal activities. I buried myself in reading *Black Beauty*. Diana went to the north grove of trees. Arthur had told her about the owl living there. She thought she might see it.

lou mandler

# Sixteen

# This Storied Land

The quiet space of the plains gives the wind room to move. Here it is easy to understand why some say it is God's breath; the wind brings a sense of those who lived on the land in other times. Sometimes it seems to be a voice from the spirit world, much like parts of the landscape, machinery, and even furniture sometimes evoke ghosts. The land is spotted with abandoned homestead shacks; with foundations marking buildings that had burned or collapsed; with clumps of trees marooned in a strip of wheat, mourning the house and barn they used to shelter. All speak of those who once lived here.

My mother often acted as midwife to bring to life our

images of the dead. Because she didn't drive, sometimes we took her out for a ride. One day when Diana and I were in high school, Diana drove Mama and me in our Kaiser to the Hanson homestead, east of our place, where my parents had lived for the first few years of their married life. Although it was only three miles east of home, I had seen it only once before, and never with my mother. That day she wore a floral housedress and her long graying hair in a bun on the back of her head. Diana and I were dressed in our usual summer jeans, our long hair caught up in ponytails.

The Hanson place wasn't much. The house was gone. The small wood-frame houses thrown up by the homesteaders in the 1920s were flimsy affairs, built with just enough lumber to hold together. They didn't resist the elements for long. The barn, sturdier and roomier than the house, had been moved to another farm, our mother said. Nothing suggesting human habitation remained but the foundation of the house. Nearby, a stand of Russian olives and some scrubby elm trees stood witness to the dreams of the long-ago owners. The June wind blew the trees and long grass. The dirt road leading to the place was nearly grown over with prairie grass; only two narrow wheel tracks remained, and the grass in the center was so tall that it noisily brushed the bottom of the car as we drove in.

Once there, we climbed out of the Kaiser and stood gazing at the abandoned farmstead surrounded by plowed and planted fields. Diana and I looked at what was there. My mother's eyes showed that she was seeing what had been there.

"You know, they said this place was haunted," she said after a bit. She grinned, her eyes gleaming. "Daddy and

I wallpapered one of the bedrooms not long after we moved in, and when we had company for supper a couple days later, we could hear the drying wallpaper cracking in the other room. We explained to the company what the noise was, but evidently they didn't believe us because a few days later we heard there were stories going around about the ghosts making noises in our bedroom." She took a minute for one of her nearly soundless giggles. Then . . .

"One thing I do know is that Old Man Hanson had a still here. One of the bedrooms really smelled of spirits. There was a story about the vet going in to the drugstore to get some alcohol, and the druggist didn't have any. The vet said he might have something that would be a good substitute. 'I've got some shine out in the rig,' he said. The pharmacist tested the moon and said he couldn't get any better alcohol. But the vet wouldn't tell him where he got it." She giggled again.

"But why did they think the place was haunted?" I asked. Now she looked into her memory more soberly.

"They said that Old Man Hanson's daughter came back as a ghost to plead with her father to let her come home."

We were silent. She paused as if to consider whether she should share such a story with her daughters. But she couldn't help but go on. First came the "Well" that marked the beginning of so many stories. Then she told us about gruff Old Man Hanson, whose oldest daughter at sixteen was pretty and hard-working, but starved for excitement, attention, and love, and who was persuaded to say yes to a good-looking young man on her father's threshing crew. Some threshing crews were made up of local men, but Old Man Hanson had hired a traveling crew who had started working the harvest in the south and followed the ripening wheat north.  When the threshing was finished at the Hanson's, the threshing crew and the young man moved on up to Canada.

The time came when Gladys Hanson could no longer hide her swelling belly, and her father reacted as some of the righteous feel they must.  He disowned the sinner.  Threw her out of the house.  She went south to Medicine Lake, but although it was only a half-day's ride in a buggy, she never saw her parents again.  In the spring, as her father was planting his crops for the fall threshing, she died in childbirth.  At threshing time, they said her ghost began appearing to him.

My mother gave a last look to the green fields and the windswept grass where the house and barn had stood.  She grimaced and said, "A terrible thing."

The regret and sadness I felt that day came over me again over thirty years later when I stood in a little Lutheran cemetery not far from the Hanson place and discovered a neglected, unmarked grave in the corner of the graveyard, on the margin of the Hanson plots.

Other pieces of land had other stories.  Even our farm machinery and our furniture had stories.  My father didn't buy new vehicles, machinery, or furniture; he found what we needed at auction sales.  We sat on chairs bought at the Barnes's sale, after they died in an auto accident.  The Petersons gave us our worn leather couch.  In the farmyard, the Minneapolis Moline tractor bore a particularly poignant reminder of a tragedy that occurred in the wheat strips we could see to the south and west of our farm.  On the high fender to the left of the tractor's driving platform, a raised, burned section stood out.

It was my brother who first told me what the rough, irregular circle was.  My father had bought the yellow tractor at Oscar Smith's auction sale. Oscar Smith was a young, likeable man who had been married just two years. He taught school in Hunter to supplement his farming income. One summer day while he was out summerfallowing, a terrible thunder and lightning storm hit. My father, working in a nearby field, stopped his tractor and crouched underneath it until the worst of the storm had passed. Perhaps Oscar Smith didn't have time to make such a decision.

When he didn't return home at dark, his young wife asked the neighbors to look for him. It didn't take long to find the tractor in the field where Oscar had been working. It stood in a nearly empty slough, its huge wheels half-sunk in the soft earth. Oscar's body was still attached to the back of the tractor, caught by a work boot as he fell after a bolt of lightning had hit him. The tractor had pulled him along until it ran into the slough, got mired in the muck, and the engine ran until the gas was gone. When the lightning had struck, two silver coins in Oscar's pocket melted, and the heat of the heavens fused them to the tractor fender.

So the ghost of Oscar Smith stood with us when we stood on the platform of our yellow tractor and felt the outline created by a lightning bolt and a young farmer's pocket change. But he was a good ghost, a good man dying young.

Without our realizing it, my mother storied the land for us day by day, meal by meal. She told us about Frenchy Sturgeon who fecklessly storied the coulees to the southeast. Frenchy bought fifty horses from a man in the Malta area and he planned to resell them to local people for a profit. He was a poor planner. He bought the horses in the fall, meaning to winter them and sell them in the spring, but it was a snowy winter, and he hadn't laid in hay. The horses couldn't forage for food through the snow, and they gradually starved to death. My horse-loving mother's face was painfully contorted when she told of farmers having to shoot the horses to put them out of their misery. In fact, she couldn't mouth or vocalize the word "shoot" and took refuge in euphemism.

"My dad told about coming upon one of those horses towards the end of the winter and the poor thing, just skin and bones, snapped at him before he took care of it." When spring came, all Frenchy could do was collect the bones of the dead horses and sell them.

So we shared the land with not only animals and our neighbors, but with the ghosts of those who had storied the land before us: Indians, homesteaders, animals. Nowhere was this sense stronger than when we visited the little Hunter graveyard with my mother. We could see the graveyard, squared by its caragana hedge, from the top of Eagle Hill. A wire fence kept the livestock away from the graves. The tracks of the Soo Line lay just yards north of the gate, and as the train approached Hunter, the whistle began to sound as it passed the graveyard.

Sometimes we drove my mother the nearly two miles north to the cemetery where Newton and Nova Doyle's babies lay in a row: one, two, three, four. Mama would walk slowly through this small plot of land, pausing before one grave to comment on the sadness of the early death, before another grave to bemoan the effect of the suicide on the man's wife and daughters, and before Mr. Hunter's grave to stand in silent reverie. We could see part of the old W. D. Hunter ranch from his grave.

We didn't prod her into speech then. We had heard about Mr. Hunter's nickname for her, "Pearl," and we had

# This Storied Land

heard about how he and Mama had taken turns pumping water by hand for days during a time when the wind didn't blow to operate the windmill, and there was no water for the cattle. We knew Mrs. Hunter thought Mama worked too hard. My mother stood in the center of the graveyard. Outside the graveyard was the land she had peopled with stories. There were ghosts all around.

Decades later, I gazed out the train window at the mostly treeless plains of eastern Montana when a California man across the aisle complained, "The thing about this country is that it has no landmarks." A landmark is a place that is recognizable or important because something that people remember and talk about happened there, I thought. And I thought of Robert Frost's words about "the land. . . still unstoried, artless, unenhanced. . ." and of Jerry Ramsey, my professor, who said that the myths and legends of the Indians had storied the land long before white Americans came west to "discover" these plains. I saw my mother's focused eyes behind her glasses as she told one of the many tales that marked the windy land about sixty miles north of the scene outside my train window. My California travel-mate just didn't know about this storied land.

lou mandler

# Seventeen

# Critters

"Funny-looking critters, aren't they?" my father asked, when, in his late sixties, he saw a live lobster for the first time as he and my mother visited us in Connecticut. My father was familiar with the fowl of the air and the beast of the field, but not with the fish of the sea. Daddy classified the animals living on the prairie in much the same way he classified the birds, not by their beauty but by whether they were boon or bane to his crops and cattle. He judged the creatures of the prairie primarily by how they affected our survival.

In another, earlier time, the wild creatures had helped

him survive. During the 1930s, when some people were going on the dole, my father trapped muskrats, weasels, badger, and even skunk. During the worst years of the drought, Daddy's income for the year, $250.00, came from selling the pelts of the trapped animals. When I was a child, his traps hung on nails in the machine shed, mostly unused.

During the good farming years of the 1950s, my father could rely on domestic animals for part of our income. He built a small herd of registered Aberdeen Angus cattle, the first such herd in the county. We all absorbed and reflected my parents' pride in the black cattle who grazed our pastures. My mother expressed her pride; my father didn't, but his was obvious. My mother carefully recorded the cattle purchases, births, deaths, and sales in a big black book.

Mama's even script in the black book documents some of the challenges of developing the Angus herd. A problem cow was soon sold. A cow who tried to crawl under the barbed wire fences was definitely a problem cow. The black book notes of Pride Queen of Eagle Hill, "Good cow but fence crawler—sold Sidney, Nov. 25th, '59." Ever Eola of Airyland met the same fate: "Sold fall 1956—Kinda small but good type—sold her because she was a fence crawler, early maturing calves."

Sometimes my father tried to cure a fence crawler by putting a "poke" on the cow, a triangle he welded together out of metal fence posts and put on the cow's neck. But at least once this backfired. My mother's note on Queen Lassie of Eagle Hill reads, "Summer of '56 found dead in slough—we think she was struck by lightning, had a poke on."

Sometimes a cow was lost because of accidents of nature, genetic fate, or the cow's appetite. My mother wrote about Eagle Hill Blackbird, "Lump on jaw also calved late—reason for selling. May 21st, 1958 at Sidney." Eola Hill was "sold fall '56—stub ears." Eagle Hill Esterel "bloated and died over East, P thinks from alfalfa." Eagle Hill Beatrice also "died of bloat, Oct. 13th, 1960." Eagle Hill Lassie was sold because she was a poor mother who ignored her babies, "Three calves, vet delivered one and didn't claim. Didn't claim third. Sold."

If Daddy discovered that one of our cattle was in the early stages of the bloat, he sometimes asked Joe Morgan to come. Among Joe's talents was a skill for doctoring cattle, but sometimes his skill could not help. One of the severest financial blows to the Angus herd took place soon after my father paid two thousand dollars, an astronomical sum and a large portion of his income, for a registered Angus bull. A few weeks later, lightning struck and killed it in the pasture.

My parents kept no other animals as income producers. My mother, in her opinionated way, often expressed her scorn for the stupidity of sheep, and she felt chickens were too dirty and labor-intensive for the eggs and meals they provided. Our dogs were true farm dogs, never allowed in the house. Of course Mama's horse Snider had a place of his own in the hierarchy of farm animals, somewhere between the Angus cattle and heaven.

Actually, the chain of life on the prairie wasn't a hierarchy. A nuisance at one time might render valuable service at another time. The skunk, once a contributor to my father's income, was useful as an insect eater, but it could be a nuisance if it chose to live in the space beneath the barn. The coyote, an eerie voice in the prairie night, reminded us that our pastures were alive with animals while we slept.

During the 1930s, the coyote's pelt could supplement a hungry family's income. And as scavengers, they performed a useful service in keeping the prairie clean of rotting animal carcasses. My father didn't have an animal graveyard or use a dead animal service; he hauled carcasses to a rock pile where the coyotes, by feeding themselves, kept the prairie smelling clean. I didn't learn about the central role the coyote played in Indian myths and legends for another thirty years.

In a good gopher year, gophers were a nuisance and more because of their appetite for our precious grain. When I was a sixth-grader, the gophers were having a good year. They had dug holes everywhere—behind the house in the area where we dumped the slop bucket and the ashes from the furnace, by the gate, between the swing and the north shelterbelt, in the fields. One summer day at the noon dinner table, my father voiced a complaint about the number of gophers that summer. Always eager to please Daddy, I asked, "So, how can we get rid of them?"

"Well," he said, smiling at me. "Trap them! Set some traps, and I'll give you a penny for every gopher tail."

This wasn't a high bounty, but that my frugal father offered a bounty at all was significant. His half-joking challenge made me determined to battle our gopher problem.

Besides the muskrat traps that my brother Arthur used during the winter, a few gopher traps hung in the machine shed. I threw off the memory of the smell of the freshly skinned muskrat pelts turned skin-side-out, fur-side-in, which Arthur stretched over tent-shaped wires to dry. I knew I wouldn't be able to skin an animal, but I thought I could manage to remove the tail of a dead gopher. The task my father set seemed easy enough.

Arthur taught me how to drive the stakes and set the traps; he also offered advice on how to separate gopher and tail. Parting a gopher from its tail was like parting a sparrow from its head—both involved quick, decisive wrist movements. What Arthur left unsaid was that the trap doesn't necessarily kill the gopher, and that, in such a case, effecting death would be up to me, not the trap.

One day as I walked toward the trap I had set by the front gate, the tan shape I saw in it seemed still tensed with life. As I walked closer, the trapped gopher fixed me with his living eyes, and I saw that the trap had caught just the hind legs of the animal. I wanted to turn away from this gopher's eyes. Panic and revulsion filled my guts and rose to my throat. I wanted help, but my father and brother were both out in the fields. Diana was the only sister who would help me, but pride stopped me from seeking her out. I would handle this on my own. I couldn't let the gopher loose. I knew I had to kill it.

On a winter day, I had watched from the window as my brother, standing on the iced-over slough, stoned a trapped muskrat. I found some muskmelon-sized rocks in the prairie grass. Taking one in my right hand, I took a deep breath, aimed at the gopher, and threw it as hard as I could, closing my eyes at the last second. I turned my back for a minute to gather the strength to check my work. Then I looked at the rock, the gopher, and the trap. The sun was still shining, the wind was still blowing, the prairie grass still smelled good. The gopher was dead, but my trapping career was over.

At times other animals also threatened the farmers' survival. The jackrabbits of the prairies are not the cute little cottontails of the East. Both Mama and Daddy were apt to say about jackrabbits, "Why, they're no good." Some of the photographs in the desk drawer detailed the history of the hostility of prairie people toward jackrabbits. One large, slightly blurred photo showed a fenced area with men and young boys standing outside it, looking in at what appeared to be white snowdrifts.

"What's this?" we asked our mother.

"Those are jackrabbits," she said. "That's a rabbit drive."

She only needed a "What's that?" to go on, but it was one of the stories about a distasteful topic that she told with a pained look on her face.

We learned that during the 1930s, the jackrabbit population zoomed into the tens of thousands in the county. Jackrabbits were devouring anything that grew, and the people were not willing to give in to them. The rabbits had to go. The farmers organized a hunt, and with the town of Rostad as their destination, dozens of men and boys spread out in a semi-circle, starting at the Old Blue Trail five miles away from Rostad. Walking slowly and uniformly towards the center of the circle, they scared up scores of rabbits; as the semi-circle of hunters tightened, the rabbits were driven into a chicken-wire fence, too tall and too low to the ground for the rabbits to leap over or wriggle under.

"Oh, a few rabbits got away," my mother said. "But by the time the drive was over, hundreds of them were trapped in the fence."

"And then?" we asked. The photograph told us that the rabbits were dead. My mother had left that part out of her story.

She burst out with an abrupt "Oh!" that came with a shake of her head. Then she hesitated as she decided between truth and silence.

"They clubbed them to death," she said.

We gasped.

"In some of the drives, they shot the rabbits, but you know ammunition was scarce and it seemed a waste of it when the rabbits couldn't get away anyway. Then I s'pose the hides didn't get spoiled with the shot. You can't sell skins that are full of holes. And of course there were kids there, too. Lots of guns aren't so good with kids around."

"Was Daddy there?" we asked.

"Oh yes, it was like a grass fire. You had to help."

My father sometimes shot rabbits in the winter if they dared to nibble on the bark of the precious trees my parents had planted, but Daddy was not a hunter. He spent his off-season time in his shop, solving problems, repairing or creating machines. Our land was posted with a *NO HUNTING* sign during the fall season for those tempted to shoot the pheasant and the partridge living in our east shelterbelt. Should anyone drive into our yard to plead for a special dispensation, Daddy's response was always a calm, "Oh, I don't think so." When some of the gun-fond farmers north of Hunter shot several foxes and tied them to the fence posts along the road, Daddy grimaced and shook his head.

The acres of our farm seemed a demesne, with my father its overseeing lord. The pastures, the wheat fields, the farmyard knew his footstep. He strode into the wheat fields, checking the heads of wheat. He watched the sky, looking for rain or storms. He examined his herd, husbanding their progress. He listened, observed, and knew the life on every acre and every corner, from the height of Eagle Hill to the hollow of the buffalo round.

My mother knew the land in another way. She knew the lay of the land and she had once ridden horseback over most of it, but she knew it most truly in her mind and heart. Together my parents guarded the life on this section of the planet, and, like all deities, they sometimes sanctioned death to preserve life. My father butchered some of the cattle he fed. My mother never forgot the dog her father had to kill because the neighbors said it was killing their sheep.

They also knew there was a place where their guardianship ended, where mystery begins. That place can be heard in the cry of the coyote, seen in the thrilling expanse of owl wing coming through the twilight, hinted by the fresh dirt outside the hole of the badger who never shows his face, felt in the air when a storm is brewing. My mother, in particular, loved a suggestion of wildness in domestic things. We knew Snider was better because he was part mustang. She even seemed to think in this way about people. Why else would she be so fascinated by gypsies and drawn so to stories about outlaws and adventurers?

But my mother drew a line at living in a house with certain creatures. When we were grown and my father was in his seventies, he fulfilled a dream of building a house into the side of the hill across the road from the "new" house he had built in the early 1950s. This earth house's southern exposure caught the warming winter sun; it provided protection against the constant wind and summer heat. When he and my mother moved into the earth house, he had neglected one detail: he hadn't put screens over the heating vents in the concrete floor. Soon ungainly, green-black salamanders crawled up through the vents to explore.

My mother discovered them one by one as, dazed by

the light and confused by the absence of good dank earth, they sluggishly worked their ugly legs in search of dark and clamminess. One of these invading amphibians made it down the hall nearly to my parents' bedroom before my mother spotted it. My father was not offended or alarmed by these intruders. He calmly scooped them up in the dust-pan and deposited them outside where they could find a comfortable dark.

"Why, they won't hurt you. They're just lizards," he said.

My mother was indignant at his refusal to get excited over the lizard invasion. "Yeah," she said to the damp-skinned creature heading toward their bedroom, "You go right in there and get in bed with him and see how he likes it."

Soon after, my father installed screens over the vents.

lou mandler

# Eighteen
# A Dry and Thirsty Land

When I was growing up, successful farming seemed to depend on my father's wisdom and work, but also on the forces of earth and sky. Sometimes the earth nurtured millions of grasshopper eggs that hatched into voracious wheat-eating insects. Sometimes wild oats or mustard weed grew so vigorously that the weed choked out the cash crops of wheat, barley, or flax. And sometimes the sky played the cruel game of hurling wheat-crushing hail at the earth. More often, it refused to let rain come down.

Water—that most sacred, most scarce element—was desired, measured, and saved as if it were gold. To the end of her life, every summer my mother made sure barrels were positioned under the downspouts to catch rainwater for washing hair and clothes and watering the garden. She refused to own an automatic washer because she felt it wasted water.

In the Farm Record book my mother kept for the 1937 growing season, the month of May has "NO RAIN" written across both pages. The other entry for the month is "Barley on west patch seeded May 22nd, hardly any moisture." The month of June bears the same "No Rain" note. In July, "Corn not doing so bad—but needs rain awful bad." Then: "First rain of the season on Sunday, July 11th, water standing around. Second rain, Tuesday the 13th. A good downpour that lasted three-quarters of an hour. Barley beginning to sprout Tuesday before rain, put in May 22nd."

Our parents lived half their lives with their eyes on the skies, checking for a suggestion of rain. The rain gauge measured our welfare. Each tenth of an inch mattered. When we went to convention or Sunday morning meeting, some of the verses the farmers read from the Bible exactly suited the promises we all yearned for: *I will. . . give you the rain of your land in his due season, the first rain and the latter rain, that thou mayest gather in thy corn. . . And I will send grass in thy fields for thy cattle. . .(Deut. 11)*

Sometimes we heard threats from the Bible that described our weather: *The Lord shall make the rain of thy land powder and dust, from heaven shall it come down upon thee. . .(Deut. 28)* It was hard not to think the rain would come if somehow someone did something right.

The water in the potholes and sloughs in our pastures and fields usually evaporated before summer's end. In a good year, the melting snow of the spring thaw filled these natural depressions. In June and early July, pink and white slough flowers obscured the shallow water. By August, the water had dried up and my father cut the dried marshy grass for hay.

While they lasted, these water-filled hollows gave few of the pleasures of the mountain lakes we had seen in the Rocky Mountains. If we went wading in slough water, we were apt to get the parasite called "swimmer's itch" or discover a dozen bloodsuckers, or leeches, attached to our legs. We never learned to swim. That my father could swim and ice skate enlarged his stature in our eyes. If the big slough was very full, my brother supervised building a raft out of wooden fence posts, and we poled around in the shallow water. This fun lasted until the sloughs began to dry up and there wasn't enough water to float our raft.

Science helped provide a water supply more lasting than sloughs. After the wind and dry earth worked together to create giant dust storms in the 1930s, the Soil Conservation Service encouraged new farming methods—strip farming, crop rotation, summerfallowing, shelterbelts. And dams. In each of our pastures, the Soil Conservation deepened natural hollows to create dams that hold snow run-off and rain water throughout the summer and into the fall. Mimicking Daddy, we called the dam in our west pasture "Mama's dam" for the same reason we called the section of land east of Eagle Hill "Mama's land"—because she was the moving force behind acquiring the land and improving the water supply. The surface over the deeper water of the dam was not disturbed by slough grass, and we skipped rocks in the top inches of water, holding contests to see who could skip a rock the greatest distance.

The Soil Conservation's scientific methods made our thirsty land more fecund, but before long, we discovered it wasn't always lack of rain that threatened our crops and livestock. Sometimes the advances of science brought not life, but death.

My brother Arthur was a rambler. When he wasn't reading or working for my father, he roamed the pastures. A one-person Lewis and Clark to Diana and me, he would return from his walks and lure us out with reports of a duck nest, a dead cow in the slough, a strange and wondrous rock formation in the neighbor's pastures. One early summer day, he burst into the house with an excited report of epidemic death.

"There are all kinds of dead things around the dam!" he said.

Diana and I followed him on a run about a quarter mile away in the east pasture to the dam beside the road. As we came near, our footsteps slowed in a terrible awe. We took a few more steps and just stood, our eyes taking in a drift of green, white, and brown death ringing the dam. Dozens of dead frogs, a few turtles, some baby ducks, water snakes, and even a couple otters and muskrats lay in a circle just at the edge of the water. We'd never known that the dam had nourished such plentiful life, and now the hidden creatures of the water showed us, by dying, that they had lived.

Why? How? What? We thought we were pretty smart kids and could usually figure things out, but we came up with no answers for this sad scene. The dam water had somehow turned against the life within it and discharged each and every living thing in an undiscriminating mass death. We could only circle the water and count the carcasses by category.

So it was that we had a complete report for my father when he came home for dinner at noon. His thoughts immediately went beyond our description of devastation to what still lived. His cattle. The polluted dam was the water supply for the cattle in the east pasture.

I don't remember how my father coped with this. I do remember my mother telling us just how this wholesale death in the water occurred. She put the fault on the huge oil trucks that roared past our farm, bearing derricks and drills. When the trucks first began driving up and down our gravel road, we chattered excitedly about the possibility of oil being discovered on our land. The oil company soon drilled a test well near Rostad, and we saw the lights on the derrick piercing the lonely night sky, the larger world intruding into our country. When we drove over for a closer look, we thought we were as close as we would ever be to oil exploration. We were wrong.

The driver of one of the oil trucks had dumped a truckload of salt water into our dam. It killed all the life in the dam's fresh water. Later, when a test well was drilled on our land, a couple of our cows died from exposure to some lead carelessly left behind by the workers.

Just as the need for water on big cattle spreads inspired some of the violent and bloody range wars more than fifty years before, so the need for water brought the benefits and hazards of science to small dry-land farms in the 1950s. In the effort to coax more bushels of wheat from our dry and thirsty land, "science" became increasingly involved in grain production, too. Water, air, earth—all felt its effects.

One midsummer day when I was about seven, we five older children were sitting on the entry-way step, away from the hot sun, when we heard the roar of an engine. It came not, as usual, from the fields but from the sky, and looking up, we saw our first airplane. None of the pictures we had seen prepared us for the actual sight and sound of this fly-shaped machine. It was flying so low we could see the wheels, the cockpit. My mother called for us to come inside. We resisted. She insisted. She won.

Inside, we crowded around the window, questioning and exclaiming as the plane repeatedly banked, turned, and returned. We learned from our mother that our neighbor had hired a crop duster to treat the weeds and wild oats in his fields. We thrilled to the novel sight of the cumbersome machine noisily making its way through the air while a fine dust fell from it to earth.

My father watched the crop-dusting plane with great curiosity. He was a cautious man. When nearly all the children in the country were being vaccinated against polio, my father took a wait and see attitude. (I wasn't vaccinated against polio until I entered Montana State University.) Now he began his deliberations. As the months unfolded, it became apparent that our neighbor's crops were, indeed, more weed-free, but the grove of trees, all that remained of an old homestead near the fields, didn't form leaves the next year. My mother said the crop-duster's visit killed the trees.

As time passed, my father did enter the chemical age of farming. At first, he hired not a duster, but a crop sprayer. To mark where the pilot should spray, Daddy and my brother held flags at the ends of the crop strips. They didn't know then about the dangers of the spray mist drifting down upon them from the air. Soon, my father and all our neighbors were using insecticides and herbicides, and each farmer's pickup sported a spray rig. In time, Daddy must have read and heard about the hazards of chemicals, and he began exercising his characteristic caution again. In the way he kept us from harm by walking us though blizzards and keeping us away from moving machinery, he didn't let us near his sprays and pesticides. Only my father mixed and dispensed the poison for his spray rig.

Other fathers were not so careful. Once Arthur, Diana, and I met a teenage school friend on the road near the Hunter graveyard. We stopped to talk. His hands were dirt-covered, and as we watched with disbelief, he casually opened the spigot of the weed sprayer on his pickup and washed his hands in the poisonous mix.

By the early 1960s, science worked beside the nature gods to influence farmers' fortunes. With the use of insecticides and herbicides and moisture conserving farming methods, the harvests yielded more bushels of wheat. Maybe our dry ground could become a wellspring. But on Pete and Iling Bertelson's farm north of Hunter, colon cancer cut into the family. First their daughter Sharon's husband died. Then Pete. Then Sharon. Iling survived her cancer treatment; so, too, has Iling's granddaughter, Sharon's daughter. Perhaps science brought the cancer, perhaps nature did. No one knows.

I can still see the drift of death that the saline water produced when it was dumped into our fresh dam water. A mile to the west, a grove of dead trees remembers a machine rumbling above, showering it with a fine dust. I remember, too, my father's face as he sat on the floor within the open garage door of his shop. It was raining after a long dry spell. His body was tensely still; his face showed joy for the rain, and fear that it would be only enough to settle the dust. That fervent hope mingled with fear, I thought, is what makes farmers use scientific methods to ensure a good harvest and what, long ago, made people dance for rain.

lou mandler

Part Three

# Harvest

lou mandler

# Nineteen

# Patterns for Life

Mama usually kept my parents' bedroom door locked, saying it was one place in the house the kids couldn't go. One day in my early adolescence, perhaps by devious means, I found myself alone in their room. I explored this forbidden place with my eyes. It wasn't that exciting. Bed with rumpled spread, chest of drawers covered with odds and ends, straight-backed chair with an empty glass on it—all showed my mother's casual habits. Then I glanced at the two doorless closets, one for each parent. Arrested by the very different pictures they displayed, I sat down on the bed and stared at them.

I could see my father's careful eye and deliberate hands creating the order I saw in his closet. The blue workshirts hung as neatly as the couple of finely striped dress shirts next to them. In the section Daddy had allotted to pants, all were hung with their legs ending at the same place. An extra pair of work boots and his black dress oxfords stood in a precise line on the floor. A new gray felt dress hat sat squarely beside an older, boxier and darker one.

My mother's closet took some studying to make sense of it. Books and bags had been thrown helter-skelter onto the top shelf. Below it, two or three "meeting" dresses hung haphazardly. One was a dress I hated—Elvira Thompson's navy and white polka dot, given to Mama when Elvira had died. I couldn't believe my mother would wear a dead woman's dress. Added to the visual cacophony were an old coat, my little sister's outgrown pink organdy dress, and a fancy apron for convention. A packet of old letters, a small stack of old magazines, a stash of Kleenex packets, and a single black-laced shoe were visible on the closet floor. Perhaps the other shoe was lurking behind the overalls to be mended. I investigated the books peeping out from this accumulation. One looked like the kind my mother read but felt was too worldly for her children. I tucked it under my arm.

My parents were as different as their closets. My father, in his workplace of sun and open air and order, worked at making sense of things with reason and design. My mother's spirit infused us with an appetite for life despite her regular encounters with suffering. The difference between work and pleasure was sometimes difficult to discern in the life patterns we observed.

# This Storied Land

Pleasure was the sight and sound of clean clothes whipping on the clothesline, of knowing that tomorrow would be a sunny day and the rest of the mowed hay could be baled up. Pleasure was my father successfully welding a broken disc so the summerfallowing could continue; it was my mother seeing her children come home from school to devour her warm spice cookies. As little children we played the games of childhood, but as we grew, pleasure expanded to include the jokes we told as we stacked hay, the pop songs and disc-jockey chatter we listened to as we cleaned house on Saturday nights after our parents were in bed. The dark joy of reading seemed sinful because it had nothing to do with work.

The bright pleasures of productivity didn't come easily for my mother. Each year seemed as much a pattern of sicknesses for Mama as a pattern of the seasons of nature. Then we didn't think to ask for a name for her illnesses, but some of these bouts must have been flare-ups of the gall bladder trouble for which she eventually had surgery.

Sometimes Mama's illnesses annoyed us. Sometimes they worried us. Sometimes they truly frightened us. One winter day when we were still living in the original homestead house, we were gathered around the breakfast table, eating oatmeal, my parents at either end. In these days right after my parents decided to become part of The Truth, my mother let her dark, wavy hair grow longer, but her unruly hair resisted the neat rolled arrangements favored by women in The Truth. Like her own nature, her hair didn't take well to confinement, and rather than struggle with it daily, she usually folded a bandana on the bias and bound it up, tying the bandana ends at the top of her head.

That winter day she was wearing a print housedress

# lou mandler

and, with her hair bandana-bound, had seated herself at the table. Suddenly, she put one elbow on table's edge, her hand to her face, and uttered my father's name, "Philip!" As we six children stared at her, she moaned, her eyes rolled up, and she slumped over. My usually slow-moving father sprang to her end of the table in time to catch her before she fell to the floor. He carried her into the front room and closed the door. We abandoned our oatmeal and huddled in the corner, our eyes wide with questions and fear. After a time, Daddy emerged, and we looked our fearful questions at him. "Mama fainted. She'll be all right," he said. "We better get you kids to school."

We wondered whether we should believe Daddy's assurances, and our anxiety did its work. Arthur threw up in school that day. Talkative Vivien was very quiet. There were shadows in my thinking. We returned home from school that afternoon with anxious thoughts. Would Mama be there? Mama was there, somewhat quiet but with welcoming eyes. We hovered, bursting with questions we couldn't put to words. "Well, I guess I shouldn't do that again, should I?" she said through smiling lips. It was as if we all released our breath at once. The tightness I felt in my middle relaxed. Mama was joking. She really was going to be all right.

It seemed my mother's illnesses often struck during the winter, as if some life tonic disappeared with the harvest. Like the natural world around her, she seemed to come to life anew in the spring and summer, for the planting and harvesting seasons.

When Mama was feeling well, the kitchen became a chaotic room of activity, talk, life, laughter, work. Here my mother filled the tin bread pan with dough for six loaves of bread and placed it on the table where the sun from the south roused the yeast to life and gave the bread strength to lift the lid from the pan. Here Mama sat in July shelling, cooking, and serving the summer garden beans, peas, and corn. Sorting chokecherries. All year the jelly and syrup from these bitter, pungent berries reminded us of her summer-stained hands. Rhubarb leaves filling the slop bucket signaled early summer, and bread pudding commemorated winter days.

My mother had an eye, a sense for living things that needed protection. She herself felt protected and cushioned by the great space of air and land around us, but the wind and the sudden bursts of cold and heat of this space could kill a calf born too early in the spring or a young, tender tomato vine. She was alert to the light frosts of early September, and on those nights, she tenderly covered the vulnerable garden plants with old blankets and tarps.

Later, just before the first hard frost, my mother marshaled her kids to harvest the garden yield. First, the above-ground produce: the yellow squash, the not yet ripe tomatoes, the cucumbers. Then, as the weather grew colder, the root vegetables: potatoes, beets, and rutabagas. My mother gloried in gathering the fruit of the vine and the earth before the frost killed it. She radiated satisfaction over the tumbled piles of harvested vegetables. Then the kitchen became a steaming place full of the sights and sounds of canning. The shining clean sterilized jars. The "dings" of the lid tops to test for sealing. The wet heat of the canner, fogging my mother's glasses and curling escaped strands of her hair.

Mama also did the wash in the kitchen. Wash day began when she placed the galvanized tub on the propane stove where it fit exactly over the four flaming burners.

Halfway through the hours it took to heat, she sliced a bar of tan Fels Naphtha soap into the water. Finally, she pailed the hot water into the washing machine. Mama never overcame her horror of wasting water. One tub of soapy water cleaned all the loads, first the whites, then the light-colored clothes, the towels and sheets, and last, Daddy's work overalls and shirts, grimed with field dust, grease, and oil. When the dark gray water, thick with organic matter, was finally drained, it had truly done its work.

A sunny, breezy wash day brought either my mother or a designated child outside to hang clothes on the line, and to drink in the sun and the smell and sound of clothes drying in the wind. If the weather forced us to dry the clothes inside, the wooden racks of damp clothing made the house seem more crowded and cluttered.

As we grew, we shared Mama's work. Diana made rolls and cookies. I baked pies. Vivien organized us into a weekly housecleaning team, each sister in charge of cleaning a big room and a small room. The bathroom went with the utility room, the dining room went with the kitchen, the living room went with the halls. We even split up the duties of clearing off the table—one person did the silverware; another, the "middle stuff;" another, the plates; and another, the final cleaning of the oilcloth. We took turns doing the dishes at night. But there were some things only Mama did. Only Mama made bread. Only Mama canned. Only Mama washed clothes.

My mother's natural impulses provided a spark against the dark of her loneliness and ill health. She cooked and sorted and talked and read and laughed and willed her way to brighter times. My father, too, had a darkness to keep at bay. He sought the light by giving the world order, by fixing things, by standing resolute, by creating patterns.

His world was dictated by the seasons. He knew what anyone can know of the patterns of nature, and he created his own patterns for time and space. We shared his work, too. We never seriously believed our parents thought boys were better, but we knew my father wanted more boys to help with farm work. We responded by doing as much outside work as he asked us to. We picked rocks from the fields, sorted the cattle, rode the baler, occasionally mowed hay, and always hauled the hay bales. He didn't ask us to do the summerfallowing; my brother Arthur summerfallowed, and came home covered in field dust. Arthur helped him fence. Some things only my father did. Only Daddy milked the cows and helped them birth their calves. Only Daddy butchered. Only Daddy fixed the machinery.

My father ordered his farm as he ordered his closet. Before him, others had already imposed a pattern on the natural curve of hill and slough of the grassland we inhabited. The first surveyors used section lines to divide this country, and the straightness of power lines, fence lines, roads, and strips of cropland followed the geometric design of line and block of section divisions. Occasionally, as the road around Eagle Hill did, the roads curved in recognition of a slough or a hill. The neat strips of crop land south of the home place showed alternating black and green in spring and summer, black and gold in the fall.

Daddy kept the weeds down in the fallow fields; he pulled the rocks out of them to keep his machinery from breaking. He moved the cattle from pasture to pasture in a timely fashion. He put the bulls in with the cows at the right time: too early, and spring brings the risk of newborn calves dying in a spate of freezing weather; too late, and the calves don't weigh enough to bring a good market price.

When Daddy gave us a job, he always taught us how to do it. There was a method to most tasks. Hauling hay bales in from the field and stacking them at home was our primary summer work. It took three to bring home a load of hay, one to drive and throw the bales up onto the truck and two to stack. We started young. When I was in the third grade, I drove my first vehicle, the tractor that pulled the hayrack. In a few years the truck replaced the hayrack.

When we began using the truck, Daddy showed us how to stack. Standing in the truck box, he lined five bales, cut-side down, for the first row. They exactly fit the space of the truck box.

"See? Having the softer side up makes it easier to stand on the bales and to move the other bales around on top."

We helped him lay out another row.

"Now we're ready to start the second layer."

"Why not finish the whole first layer first?"

"You'll see."

Very soon we did see. The load had to be done in steps because the person throwing the bales up from the field couldn't throw a bale much above the second layer. Daddy proceeded to show us that the second layer was like the first, but with the bales criss-cross to the first layer.

"Why do we have to put them that way?" my sister Betsy asked. "Why not put them just like the first layer?"

"It makes the load tighter," he said.

I found if I kept the crosswise pattern of weaving in mind, it was easier to build a load of hay. The load narrowed in increments from the third to the fourth layers and finally to the fifth and sixth layers, where the top peak of the triangle was formed by single alternating bales to carry out the weaving pattern.

Struggling with prickly hay bales in the hot summer sun was a sweaty task, but we liked working outside. Shared work was a kind of communication with Daddy. We knew we could please him by doing good work. Talking wasn't necessary.

Sometimes the pictures that endure are in the mind, not photographs in a desk drawer. One summer day, my father hauled hay with us. He drove the truck and threw the bales up onto the truck box. After unloading the hay, with my two younger sisters and me standing in the truck box, he drove the truck to the driveway between the house and the granary. As soon as it stopped, my two sisters jumped out and ran to the house. My father, after turning off the motor, sat still. Separated from him by the cab but aware of his quiet presence, I, too, lingered.

It was day into evening time. There was no wind, and the softening light foreshadowed the quiet of night. I could hear each small sound distinctly, a night hawk's cry from the pasture, a meadowlark's sunset trill. A few hesitant frogs tuned up their voices. The insects murmured in the grass. Into the hush a car approached from the south, the tire on gravel sound intruding. But soon it, too, died away and the still expectation of approaching night enveloped us again. I felt the satisfaction of a good day's work done, a sense that something awesome, but not quite the God of The Truth, filled the space between earth and sky. Apart but together, my father and I remained for many minutes. When Daddy finally stirred, climbed out of the cab, and walked toward the house, I walked with him. We didn't speak.

# This Storied Land

lou mandler

# Twenty

# The Reading "Problem"

*"Favorite Toy: Books"*
—My mother's baby book,
written in her father's hand

When I was a child, we children were ashamed that our mother wasn't like other mothers. The mothers in our Mac and Muff, Bob and Nancy readers in school and later, in *Wee Wisdom* magazine, were blonde, curly-headed, and cheerful. Our mother was different from these fictional mothers and, we believed, from all the other mothers we knew. We thought other mothers kept immaculate houses, were never sick, wore high heels, and served meals on time. We knew of no other mother, in The Truth or of the Hunter community, who sometimes locked herself in the bedroom to read. We never told anyone about this terrible practice of Mama's.

My mother would read anything. As soon as we started school we learned that we had to hide any book we brought home if we wanted to read it ourselves. Mama wasn't proud. She would read third-grade books, high school library books, junior high school literature anthologies, or a *True Confessions* magazine that my sister had secretly, she thought, borrowed from a friend.

Somehow Mama made reading seem a sensuous, forbidden thing, perhaps because she read in secret. But so it was that we learned that life's experiences, sins and all, are available on the printed page. Mama sometimes abdicated her household tasks to read. When we were in high school, she would add a farewell statement just before she disappeared behind her locked bedroom door.

"You girls can fix supper tonight," she would say.

Or maybe her reading had a forbidden aura because my father didn't approve of this obsession. Oh, he read all right, openly in the front room, but his reading seemed practical, not sensual. He thought one read to get good grades, to learn the latest farming methods, to learn geography, to satisfy one's curiosity about how things work. To him, reading with abandon was an unhealthy indulgence, it disturbed the daily routine and reduced efficiency. It got in the way of work. Since we knew my father was perfect, we accepted that reading to excess was unquestionably a vice.

Some of Mama's children also had a reading "problem."

I did. My brother Arthur did. So did my sister Vivien.

And my father was right; this thirst for the dark pleasure of reading got in the way of life. One of our few inviolate family practices was that we never began a meal until all eight or nine—or however many there were in the family at the time—were seated at the table. It took tremendous self-discipline to stop reading a good book to join the family at mealtime. On occasions when everyone except one of the known readers was gathered, my father was apt to say in disgust,"Oh, she's (he's) probably reading."

Our failure to subordinate the call of a book to our real-life duties sometimes created genuine problems for my father. One very cold winter day, in a year before we moved to the new house, the mercury in the thermometer hovered below zero, and Daddy assigned my brother the task of filling the stock tank with water and monitoring the level. Arthur started the task responsibly enough. He poured hot water over the hydrant to loosen the handle. Then he put the hose in the tank and started the water. The black Angus cattle crowded around, their breaths steaming white in the air, caked manure and ice clinging to their winter hides. Now Arthur had to wait. It would take a while for fifty cattle to get their turn to drink. It was cold. And he had a good book inside. He decided to go inside for fifteen minutes and come back out in time for the last drinkers.

I, too, was reading in the darkened front room, which also served as Arthur's bedroom, when Arthur entered, threw himself on his rumpled bed, and re-entered the world of his book. Neither of us knew how much time had drifted past when Daddy's quick, angry step and disgusted scowl broke into our printed page worlds. Startled and alarmed by the unusual sight of our father's visible anger, I drew myself deep into my chair as Daddy pulled Arthur off the bed.

"Hey, what do you think you're doing? The tank is overflowing!"

My brother didn't have to be told of the sins upon his head. He had wasted water, and by creating a lake of ice in the barnyard, made it dangerous or impossible for the cattle to reach the tank the next day. All this for a book!

Reading got Arthur into other scrapes as well. When he was in high school, he always carried a library book amongst the books he took from class to class. He favored desks in the back of the room so that he could slip into the book world if he grew bored. Arthur had a great, booming laugh that exploded out of him suddenly. One day during an English class, as the teacher lectured the students on how to do the essay assignment, Arthur burst into laughter from the back of the room, where he was absorbed in a book. As an adult, he once sat reading in the Calgary airport and missed his flight to Regina.

We knew we got our reading "problem" from our mother, and we knew it was a real problem. Our logical minds therefore decided that we inherited bad things from our mother and good things from our father. We believed this for a good while.

My own reading "problem" began when I was five. One day when my older brother and sisters were in school, my father was sitting in a chair reading a farm magazine and I was sitting on the linoleum floor beside him with a Bible, the only book we owned then besides a set of medical encyclopedias. Yearning to cross the magical threshold into the world of reading, a world my brother and sisters had already entered,

# This Storied Land

I stared at a Bible page, trying to find a pattern. Finally, I isolated short words which appeared more than once on a page—*a, and, said* —and I asked my father what those words were. He pronounced the words with patience, and I resumed my search for literacy, consulting him again from time to time.

By the time I started school in Hunter, I was reading. In the year that England's King George died, Miss Tucker subscribed to *The Weekly Reader*. Weeks after his death, I read about England's new Queen in that little newspaper. I stared at the photo of Princess Anne and Prince Charles. They were close to my age. I found the texts in the Mac and Muff/Bob and Nancy readers boring, but I lingered over the illustrations. The father didn't wear overalls. The house was pretty. And then there was that cute, smiling mother.

The books in the library of our rural school were mostly nineteenth century works. *Captain January*, a slim book with a sapphire cover, gave me my first cathartic cry when the old sea captain died a lyrical, poignant death. I thought God probably looked like the illustrator's portrayal of the captain. The fanciful illustrations in *The Water Babies* and the Victorian art in *The Mother Goose Book* showed me a completely new image of humanity, of richly dressed and variously occupied people; and of nature, of climes with green vegetation and trees and flowers.

My second-grade teacher read books aloud to the entire group of sixteen students after lunch every day. We heard *The Green Grass of Wyoming* and *Assignment in Brittany*. We cried together over the tragedies in *Little Britches*. Such emotional experiences hooked me. I wanted more.

# lou mandler

By the time I went to the larger school in Plentywood as a fourth-grader, I had an entrenched reading problem. Plentywood had no elementary school library, but my classroom had a shelf of books for free reading, about half of which were turquoise-bound biographies of famous men and women, mostly men. I read them all, even the biography of Mad Anthony Wayne. But the best source for books during my fourth-, fifth-, and sixth-grade years was my sister Vivien.

Because she was four years older than I, she could take books out from the high school library. I had to compete with her and my mother for her library books, but I managed to read such books as *Cheaper by the Dozen, White Orchids,* and career romance novels about nurses and secretaries. My mother bought a set of Funk and Wagnalls encyclopedias about this time, and when I had nothing better to read, I read bits from random volumes of these black and sand colored books. It was there that I discovered a picture of Wolfgang Mozart and decided he was probably the most beautiful man who had ever lived. All the readers in our family read Zane Grey's romantic novels of the West. My mother had read them years before, but she read them again as we discovered them. Some of the town girls in my class read Nancy Drew books; I tried one, but I found the next one boring and thereafter ignored formulaic adventures of schoolgirls.

The homework my teachers assigned was usually a peripheral concern to me, and I sandwiched it between periods of reading. When I entered junior high, I could check out books from the high school library, which consisted of some shelves of books in a corner of the study hall. Scanning the title pages, touching the covers, and reading selected passages was a tactile pleasure, foreshadowing the pleasure of the reading session to come later. I discovered books by Bess Street Aldrich, Thomas Costain, Edna Ferber. For a time, I read a book a day. In the seventh grade, I started to read *Gone with the Wind*. I knew I would be lost if I brought it home the first day, so with prideful self-discipline, I rationed my indulgence, and read it only in school until I had about three hundred pages left. Then I allowed myself to bring it home, and I finished it that night.

The problem with such surrender was that I often read until two or three in the morning, and my father didn't approve of leaving the lights burning that long nor of the sleep I lost. My parents' bedroom was directly below the room I shared with Betsy, and the light from our window reflected on the snow or the ground outside their bedroom. If Daddy knew I was reading at two or three in the morning, he had a simple solution. He flipped the circuit breaker to the lights in our bedroom. I would be raptly reading an important conversation, a vital clue, or a love scene and the room would plunge into darkness. I always knew what had happened. There was no recourse but to put the book on the floor and go to sleep.

My brother Arthur went away to college when I was in the seventh grade, and when he came home for his first vacation, he brought a boxful of steamy paperbacks that he secreted in his room. Having a nose for books, I discovered them. As I raced through their pages, I also discovered that some writers described the insides of thighs and, vaguely, the sex act itself. I read on, of course.

One day while I was in the middle of one of these sizzling rags, my father came into the room, stood for a long moment with his hands in his overall pockets, and finally cleared his throat and said, "I don't think you should be reading those." I blushed, put the book back in the box, and crept away. I wondered how he knew about the content. My mother must have told him.

In my "read to the finish" style, I often spent entire summer days or weekends engrossed in a book. When I came to the end of the last page, often as darkness was falling, I felt like I was emerging from a drugged state. I had a reading hangover; still in the world of imagination, I had to struggle to become active, to talk to people, to even consider them. I felt dissatisfied with the mundane world and alone because no one else could know what I was feeling or had experienced in my private world. I loathed myself during these hangovers and wondered why I did this to myself. Why couldn't I just work and have a concrete, organized life like my sister Diana? I had depressing visions of spending the rest of my days curled up with a book in the old leather rocking chair as the winds of every season tore at the house. In my vision, my father would swat flies around me in the summer, and in the winter he would build coal fires in the fireplace. My mother would be in her bedroom reading.

Now at an age considered to be grown up, I still feel the pull of my mother's addiction. I know the conditions that create the craving—a certain kind of weather, a tension-fraught day, the couch with the lamp lit beside it, a good fire in the fireplace—and I know the risks of giving in to it. I confess with shame that I have ignored dirty dishes, unvacuumed rugs, unwashed children, and uncorrected papers to read. My children learned early that it takes more than one, "Mom! Hellooooo!" to transfer my attention from a book to them. My husband doesn't like reading at the table any more than my father did. At least I have never tried the trick

# This Storied Land

from *The French Lieutenant's Woman,* reading during sex. When I hear about the pleasures of a pastime that wasn't available to me as a child—golf, gambling, bowling—I think guiltily to myself, "I'd rather read."

lou mandler

# Twenty-one
# The Shrinking Table

Twice a day, every day of the year, our wooden table drew us together.  Some of the things we knew best had never been spoken.  This was true of our table rituals.  Neither of our parents ever said, "The meal cannot begin until everyone is at table." But it was so.

Once the words "Supper's ready!" left my mother's lips, the table-setter repeated the words to those reading or talking in the front room, called to anyone playing outside, yelled upstairs to those in the bedrooms, and we came.  No one put a hand on the flatware until everyone was assembled and we had observed a silent grace.  This noon and evening ritual did not take place at breakfast. "It's the only time Daddy and I have peace to talk to each other," was my mother's reason for letting us take our breakfasts individually.

We were only seven children before my sister Agnes left home. Susan and Grant were born after, when Agnes was twenty and twenty-five. During the heyday of my childhood, we sat three on either side of the rectangular table, its dark finish protected by various colorful oilcloths. We sat elbow touching elbow, flanking Mama and Daddy at opposite ends. Nine was a tight fit.

We had our regular places. Agnes, the oldest, sat in the middle on the kitchen side of the table where she said she was so busy passing things from one end of the table to the other that she hardly had time to eat. On either side of her, Arthur sat next to Daddy, and my younger sister Betsy sat next to Mama. Across the table, Diana, Vivien, and I were the row of three. One of us split the mealtime between eating and feeding the baby in the wooden high chair pulled up to a corner. We sat in mismatched wooden chairs. When they splintered and cracked, they were replaced with metal folding chairs until we acquired other wooden chairs from the Barnes's auction sale. For a time, Betsy, Diana, and I sat on the old wooden laundry bench; should the person on one end stand up without warning, the whole bench tilted like a see-saw, spilling the other two sitters onto the floor.

Our Sears Roebuck table served as more than a place to eat. During table-time we planned and reported work: in the summer, plans for fieldwork and garden work; during the school year, homework; during the spring, talk of calving. And always, talk of the weather. The table served as a meeting place to deliver important news. My sister Lillian's birth was announced at table. It also served as a kind of court during which we petitioned my father for permission and awaited his verdict. Could I go to the neighbors' and watch *Macbeth* on TV as my English teacher had assigned? ("Oh, I guess so, but it's probably all Hollywooded up.")

While my father was present and we were all hungry, table talk tended to be matter of fact, but when he left the table to take his fifteen-minute nap on the floor of the front room, we and my mother often lingered, and the talk unfurled into arguments, stories, and laughter. We disagreed, we argued over words, ideas; we analyzed and told stories about teachers and classmates. My mother, still at her end of the table, easily slipped into relating who was whose grandmother's cousin's husband while we made light of her ability to remember these familial connections. We teased her for her pronunciation of certain words and sounds. Her vocabulary came from reading, not from listening, and we laughed over the sound of some of what she said. She pronounced the letter "h" as "haitch," and we modified an old cowboy song to mock her, "*Oh, haitch up your horses and feed them some hay. . .*"

Sometimes our mother made us uncomfortable by shocking the Wiedeman sense of propriety that she herself had taught us to emulate. When she told us about Audrey Culstrom, a town character, losing her underwear as she walked down the street, Mama illustrated the story. Once the waistline elastic had given way and her panties had collapsed around Audrey's feet, Mama showed how Audrey stepped out of the garment with one foot, raised it with a high kick of the other foot, retrieved the offending cloth, tucked it into her pocket, and continued down the street. Mama's delight in this story showed in her flushed face and the nearly soundless giggle that accompanied her tale. We couldn't help but laugh too, but we felt duty bound to utter a properly scandalized, "Mama!"

The approval of the group gathered around our table was a powerful force in creating our collective values. We joined no clubs, never owned a TV, received no daily paper; the outside world was only a distant influence. The group scorned bragging, conceit, selfishness, pride, and self-promotion. Our rules of table—Don't be bossy. Don't brag. Don't be a show-off. Don't be mean. Don't grab—are still burned in my brain. Just as powerful was the effect of my mother's delight in stories of eccentric people, her affection for the underdog, her resounding approval of goodhearted people, her absolute loyalty to our father, and the deep sympathy she showed while recounting tragic stories.

When I was a child, it seemed as if our family would meet around our table forever. We couldn't believe any one of us would ever get married or leave home. But then Agnes graduated from high school, and in a few months, the table lost its first citizen. It was not a natural, easy departure. Agnes needed help, and my mother performed her part without hesitation. In the same way a mother bird, knowing her healthy babes must fly on their own, coaxes them out of the nest, so Mama worked to launch her first-born.

Agnes was an unlikely oldest child. She was quick to tears, fond of home, and never bossy. We argued with each other, but as I remember, not with Agnes. Her startle reflexes were always in perfect condition; we loved sneaking up behind her and hearing the shriek of alarm when we surprised her. She had always worn her long brown hair in braids, and by the time I was in the second grade, her braids had assumed a style encouraged by The Truth's emphasis on long hair. She parted it in the middle, rolled it above either temple, plaited two braids, and then wrapped and pinned the braids around her head. Agnes was to wear this hairstyle into her twenties. She had fairer, softer skin than any of us girls, and she was taller than all of us except Daddy and my brother.

As the oldest, Agnes had to do many things first, but the pioneer temperament didn't come naturally to her. Vivien, third in line after Agnes and Arthur, seemed to have what is now called the "first-born personality." Vivien faced the world with defiance and eagerness. With each little victory or conquest, we could feel her satisfaction. She seemed fearless. But it was Agnes, the meeker spirit, who had to go off to first grade in Hunter school alone after my parents kept her home until she was nearly seven. As a first-grader, she came home crying day after day because the big kids teased her for calling her father "Papa." To spare her further pain, my parents simply decided that he would henceforth be called "Daddy." The teasing stopped. And Agnes had to start high school in Plentywood alone, boarding during the week with Alice Stromberg, a single professing woman, in town while the rest of us attended Hunter School for our last year there.

Both Mama's and Daddy's educations had ended after the eighth grade, and they were pleased that their children were getting a high school education. Because of their backgrounds and our uncertain financial state, college was not even considered as a possibility for Agnes's post-high school plans. My mother saw to it that Agnes—and, in time, all her daughters—took typing and shorthand in high school. She wanted us to be able to support ourselves. When it came time to plan Agnes's career, Mama and the U.S. Postal Service joined forces.

As my parents had ordered our dinner table from Sears Roebuck, so they ordered house blueprints through the mail. In later years they enlisted the help of distant architects in planning the landscaping around the new house, and my mother used the mail to locate and buy a registered Welsh Corgi. Mama always ordered our school clothes from the big three catalogs—Sears-Roebuck, Montgomery-Ward, and Alden's. Our first radio was a rose-colored Alden's model. And now my mother worked with my sister Agnes to get her a mail-order job.

In Agnes's senior year in high school, Mr. Goetz's shorthand students took a test that the State of Montana sent to high schools throughout the state in an attempt to find qualified office workers. Once the test results were scored, some students were invited to apply for State office jobs as they became available. Glasgow, Scobey, and Wolf Point were among the possible job sites, and Agnes thought she might like to work in Scobey or Wolf Point, each a couple hours from home. She sent in the necessary forms. When the list of open positions came back in the mail a couple weeks later, two jobs were listed. They were both in Helena, over five hundred miles away from our remote part of the state. Agnes hesitated, but our mother saw this as an opportunity. When Mama decided something should happen, she cajoled, persuaded, and plotted until it happened. We all knew that when she set her jaw, pursed her lips, and narrowed her eyes, we could protest, but we weren't likely to win.

By November, Agnes had packed her two mail-order graduation suitcases, and my father, mother, and little sister undertook a rare automobile journey to deliver Agnes to Helena. Once established there, she took a train to visit home two or three times a year, arriving and departing from the station fifty miles south of our farm. At the end of these visits, just before the trip to meet her return train to Helena, Agnes would sit at her old place in the middle of the supper table and pass dishes to the right and left as she always had done. The meal would have just begun when her tears started to flow. We would finish our meal in silence, made speechless by her silent weeping. We didn't understand. Helena sounded like a much more exciting life than ours. Agnes worked for the State of Montana for more than thirty years.

In her first year away, our dreamy, funny brother Arthur was a senior. We didn't think about what he would do after high school. He liked books too much to be a natural farmer, but my father certainly hoped Arthur would join him in the farming life. Arthur's senior year was also the year that Plentywood High School began giving the ACT test to all seniors. One day in early winter, my parents received a phone call (by now we had a phone) from Mr. Wollan, Plentywood's Superintendent of Schools. He asked if my father would come in to discuss Arthur. Arthur had always preferred reading books to doing homework, and he avoided the really unpleasant assignments. He had even purposely missed the school bus on the day he was scheduled to give a speech in English class. Once in grade school, he had thrown his math book out the schoolroom window so he wouldn't have to do math any more. Mr. Wollan's invitation to visit couldn't be good. My father wore a worried expression, his dress hat, and his usual clean town clothes that day.

In my mother's account of Daddy's visit with Mr. Wollan, she reported that Mr. Wollan said to Daddy, "You send that boy to college." Arthur had scored at the top of his class on the ACT. We were all astonished. Arthur was really that smart? Our parents faced a dilemma. College cost money that they didn't have. Besides, college wasn't for people like them. But once again, my mother considered her child and his future, and she settled that future in her mind.

Somehow, Arthur went to college. My father gave him some cattle to sell for part of his tuition each year. He worked long hours in the dormitory cafeteria. He went to MSU in Bozeman, for two quarters, from September through March each year, and came home for the spring and summer farm work. Nine years later, he earned a degree in veterinary medicine from Washington State College.

For each of three succeeding years, our table lost a member. After Arthur went to college, my sister Vivien followed Agnes to Helena, where my mother had established, through Agnes, a launching pad for the rest of her daughters. With the exception of Susan, the youngest girl, each of Mama's seven daughters lived for a time with Agnes in Helena. It wasn't until I, the middle child, had completed high school that my mother began to try to hold on to her children. But that was six years after Agnes was the first to leave our table.

# This Storied Land

lou mandler

# Twenty-two
# Threshold Years

In my childhood, we knew our parents worked hard at protecting us from physical harm. They also kept us from anything too worldly or too violent. After I was grown, a former farm neighbor wrote to me, "We always thought your folks were too protective of you girls."

Farm children often brag that the mysteries of sex and birth are revealed to them as they observe cattle, dogs, or sheep copulating and giving birth. We had seen our bulls mounting the cattle, and we knew when calving time came, but Daddy, alone, ushered the calves into life when they needed an attendant. When I worked up the courage as a small child to ask my mother where human babies came from, she was embarrassed, but she gave me an answer. Although my mother loved to talk, she didn't speak freely about sex. But she didn't take refuge in pretty little stories to explain sex and birth. Just as we never believed in Santa Claus, so there was no talk of storks or God bringing babies. Whether it was Mama's discomfiture or my stupidity that muddled our communication, for awhile I thought babies came out through the belly button. Despite such confusion or awkwardness, none of us was in the dark for too long about the origin of babies.

My teenage years were bracketed by the birth of my sister Susan when I was thirteen and the birth of my brother Grant when I was eighteen. In the space between, I and my nearest siblings negotiated adolescence. Five years before Susan's arrival, my sister Lillian had been nearly a ten-pound baby, and Mama had hemorrhaged so badly after the delivery that the doctor was alarmed. My mother seemed worried about bringing her next child into the world. We worried, too. The fall Susan was due we took turns cleaning the kitchen and making the evening meal, and Mama spent long periods in her bedroom. Our worry didn't keep us from feeling some resentment over what we felt were unreasonably heavy household chores, and we often grumbled over our dreary life as we heated water to wash and rinse a sink full of dishes.

Whatever precautions my mother and her doctor took together, they worked. Susan's birth weight was under eight pounds. There was little hemorrhaging. My mother came home from the hospital thinner and paler, but she soon regained her spirit.

We were always aware that most local families did not have as many children as ours did. When I arrived at school

# This Storied Land

the morning after Susan was born and announced her birth, a friend said to me, "Gee, you better tell your dad to slow down." Even though Mama had difficulty with her pregnancies and deliveries, we picked up no signs of dismay from my parents about having eight children. In fact, the first clue we had that Susan was coming was a wordless exchange of smiles and blushes between my parents.

The Truth also circumscribed our teenage lives. TV, movies, dancing, make-up, short hair, indecent dress, and, of course, drinking were out of the question. There were no proms for us. We talked among ourselves about the irony that our parents were stricter than many parents in The Truth yet we didn't go to meeting. Worldly people looked at us as outsiders because they thought we belonged to "that weird religion," but people in The Truth looked at us as outsiders too. We felt we truly fit in only at home.

When my brother Arthur, a strong six-footer, was a senior, the football coach prevailed upon him to go out for football, and we were surprised and delighted when my father allowed him to do so. That year, for the first time, we went to the high school football games, and even my father attended some. However, my mother vetoed my request to try out for the school play before it reached my father's ears. We asked to be excused from phys-ed during the folk-dancing unit. But we had a radio.

Certainly my parents bought a radio to hear grain reports, the news and the weather forecast, but when we could, we spirited it away to an upstairs bedroom to listen to music.

My husband once expressed surprise that we were allowed to listen to Elvis Presley. His Catholic parents thought Elvis and his hips were immoral. It isn't that we were allowed to. We just did it, and this is one pleasure my mother closed her eyes to and our father didn't witness. Nevertheless, we couldn't see what Elvis did with his hips; his sensual voice entered our farm home over our rose-colored radio. Elvis and Johnny Horton and Farron Young and Hank Williams and Hank Snow and Tennessee Ernie Ford were all a very big deal for us.

Some of us took to our constricted way of life more naturally than others. My lean and athletic sister Diana focused her determination and love of detail on her school work. She earned the best grades in the family. My companion and inspiration in play and outside farm-work, Diana competed with me in grade school sports contests. Diana was true blue, modest, hard-working, coordinated, and strong. And good. She was so good I couldn't stand it sometimes. Diana didn't have to think about what she would do when she graduated. Mama engineered her path into college. In the way Mama thought, the class salutatorian went to college. After her college graduation, Diana taught fifth grade in Helena and then began a life as a rancher's wife.

It was my sister Vivien who perhaps struggled the most to find acceptable ways to express the stirring appetites and quickened curiosity of the teenage years. Vivien was the storyteller of our generation, always in the center of our bedroom gab sessions. It was she who had worried our parents when she became the first one of us to have a boyfriend, Kurt Jensen, when she was just a seventh-grader. As a high school girl, she spent hours putting her thick dark hair in curlers and coaxing it in a long reverse page. Vivien rolled the bottoms of her jeans just so and carefully arranged the collar of her plaid shirt. She used her considerable talents to beautify our utilitarian world as much as she could.

By that time, Mama had given up buying our clothes for us. She gave each of us a specific amount of money every fall to get our school clothes, not counting underwear, socks, and coats. At first the amount was twenty dollars each, and we spent hours combing the catalogs, and making lists: a white blouse from Sears for $1.99, a sweater and skirt, $3.99 each. We sewed skirts and wore each other's clothes to make it through the week without wearing the same outfit twice. But Vivien wasn't content with such a modest wardrobe, and she had a small, extra income. She punched lunch tickets at school, the first in a string of five Wiedeman girls to hold that job; and she was the favorite babysitter for the Hunter depot agent's children.

Vivien sewed like no one else. She sewed herself a blue satin princess-style dress and gleefully found blue suede shoes to match, an outfit not appropriate for school, but where else could she wear it? She made a yellow circle felt skirt and bought a black angora sweater to go with it. Vivien transformed the bedroom she shared with my sister Diana by sewing a skirt for the orange crate "dresser" and a matching gathered cover for the cheap fold-out bed. Baling twine served as cording.

I never heard about Vivien's ACT scores. Perhaps Mr. Wollan just didn't think it was necessary to advise the parents of a female to "send that girl to college." In any case, Vivien left home eagerly in the fall after her high school graduation and joined Agnes in Helena, going on to become an executive secretary in insurance companies in Helena; St. Paul, Minnesota; and California before her marriage.

Our physical isolation and the constraints of The

Truth affected us deeply as adolescents, but our parents themselves were more powerful forces. Mama's influence in shaping our world was pervasive. We didn't revere our mother when we were young. She was too human: she showed her emotions; she got sick; she was stubborn; she scolded us; she was sometimes improper. She often chose to read instead of work. When we were children, we were too much with Mama to know truly how we felt about her. We did revere our father.

*At one point in the first years of our marriage, my husband said to me, "Sure, your father is a nice man, but he comes in the room and you all practically prostrate yourselves. And the man barely speaks. I don't get it."*

When, as an adult, I tried to understand how a man who "barely speaks" achieved such stature, I came to realize that it was because we saw him through Mama's eyes. It was she who transferred to us her respectful and protective feelings for Daddy. We accepted the restrictions of our teenage years because it was unthinkable to disobey Daddy. We said we were afraid to, but it was really an odd mixture of wanting his respect and wanting to protect him from pain and trouble, even the kind of trouble caused by whining, restless teenagers.

Because we saw our parents as so different from each other, we privately speculated about their marriage, that shared area no outsider can know. We knew what my mother thought of my father, and he showed that he loved her, but he spoke no words to confirm that. That our father could use words in a non-practical way we knew because my mother had shown us a couple of poems he had written as a young man. They were light and humorous. One was written in honor of his brother's marriage, and the other titled, "The Windmill" began, "The windmill is no lazy cuss,/ It does its work and makes no fuss."

After my mother's death, as I sorted through what she left behind, I came across a tattered page of a letter, more than a half century old, from my father to my mother. Part of the page had been ripped away but what remained gave a voice to my father's love. Evidently they had had a lover's quarrel over attention not being paid, and he made vows regarding that. There was another issue, "Your folks have been as nice to me as I could expect, but. . . " he wrote. The next part of the letter was torn off, but the closing words were still readable, "If you don't think I should come to see you any more, I won't. But I want you to know you will always have a warm place in my heart, and I can't even tell you how much I would miss you."

Susan's birth wasn't the only important event in the fall of my thirteenth year. Grandpa and Grandma Olson moved away to Kalispell in October, near Emily and Hans Olmquist, though we were only barely aware of it. Kalispell, on the western side of the Continental Divide, had a milder climate, and as we would learn, Grandma Olson's energy was well suited to town living. In the early years on their farm, neighbors lived close together, and she didn't have far to go to visit people or know their business. When the farms became larger and neighbors farther apart, Grandma Olson's urge for gathering and spreading the news must have been terribly frustrated.  Kalispell seemed a natural setting for their retirement.

Their move across the state must have been a significant event for my parents, who had lived for fifteen years with the ominous sense of "her" living just over the hill.  No longer did they have to worry about coming face to face with her on the street in Plentywood.  My mother's brother Carl continued to live on and work the Olson farm, but he did not loom as black a psychological cloud as "she" did.  My mother must have had conflicting emotions about her parents' move west.  Whatever feelings of scorn, anger, and hurt that her mother roused in her, Mama loved her father.

*When my sister Vivien visited Grandma and Grandpa Olson in Kalispell in the 1960s, Grandpa Olson said to Vivien about our mother, "Lucy was my pet, you know."*

*Decades later my aunt Emily wrote to me, "When my dad was so very sick, and your sister Diana came up to see him, he was so happy.  He thought it was Lucy."*

My mother never saw her father again.

Our grandparents' departure to Kalispell didn't change our life much, but we were aware that some of the tension about the Olsons began to dissipate.  In a few years my younger sisters and brother rode the school bus into Plentywood with Carl's children, and the cousins began to talk together on the phone.  Carl's wife Laura brought us a peace offering of a Christmas tree, not knowing that we, following the custom of The Truth, did not decorate a Christmas tree.  The tree stayed outside in the snow.  Mama and Carl's relationship had been frozen too long to be easily repaired, but Laura's visit contributed to its gradual softening.

The partial thaw in family relations did not bring with it a revelation of what had caused the ice in the beginning. My parents continued to be close-mouthed about the family events of 1942. By then, the break was so enshrouded in years of secrecy that no one tried to discuss it. But the ghost of Grandma Olson affected us in ways we didn't know.

*Once when I was going through a questioning, rebellious time in college, my mother wrote to me, "You know, you inherited much, much of this—babbling, hysterical, impulsive behavior—from your Grandma Olson. I suppose you should have known this before, but I never really thought you had it before. So you better fight it."*

These strong words at last revealed the fear that must have been working in Mama as she hovered over our development. What if blood shows? What if one of us turned out like her mother?

When I, the fifth Wiedeman, showed up in our high school, I immediately confronted the power, responsibility, and restraint a family name can wield. I resented being typecast as a nice kid and a good student just because I bore the Wiedeman name. Although embarrassing my family was unthinkable, I fantasized about doing forbidden things. The boy I watched from my protected place in life wore a black leather jacket, combed his dark hair Elvis-style, clicked the metal caps on his shoes when he walked, and went downtown at noon so he could smoke a cigarette.

I read some Emerson and Thoreau and became passionate about their idealism. I followed the world news and wrote a heated letter full of my opinions on the Cuban missile crisis to my brother at college. I sported a "Pat for First Lady" button and had arguments with my mother, who planned to vote for Kennedy. I suffered mightily from reformist zeal and decided the only way to reform the world was to become a foreign diplomat. As a student, I was more an Arthur than a Diana, but I edited the school newspaper and was active on the fringes of school.

These were the years my mother spoke of with nostalgia decades later. In the last years of her life, part of my Saturday ritual was to call her on the phone. During one of those visits, I asked her almost idly, "What were the happiest years of your life?" She was quiet for only a moment. Then she said, "The first years of marriage. And the years when all you kids were home and involved in school, doing things. And when Grant was born."

She always enjoyed our school talk at supper, and she reveled in any honor bestowed on us. We were a sight of the life she had missed. It was during these years that Snider died. My sister Vivien remembers my mother going through "a quiet time" afterwards. I, in callow adolescence, paid little heed.

During my senior year in high school, I anticipated leaving home with a burning eagerness. Believing in action, planning, and ideas, I had decided that I was going to college, so I researched colleges. I wanted to go to a distant school in the "real" part of America. Either the University of Wisconsin or George Washington University would do, I decided, so I filled out admission applications and student loan papers and mailed them. As I lay waiting for sleep in the bed I shared with my sister Betsy, I pictured myself on a college campus in a very populated city. I was accepted at both colleges and given loans.

In February of that year, my mother called me into her bedroom. This was unusual. We stood inside her bedroom door. I waited for her to speak. Instead, she wrote a note on one of the little spiral notebooks she kept in odd places around the house. Her note read, "I am pg." Startled, I looked at her. She was smiling and blushing. Then she told me that her doctor had advised her to have gall bladder surgery before the pregnancy advanced any further. She would be entering the hospital the following week.

This would be Mama's ninth child, and she would be forty-four when delivery day came. Her hair was nearly white, her figure matronly. My mother had always made it a point never to tell anyone she was expecting until she started to show, and then she would refuse to give her due date. I witnessed a well-intentioned woman in The Truth ask her once, "When are you due, Lucy?"

"Oh, in the fall," was my mother's breezy response.

This time, however, she told me that the baby was expected in September. She didn't ask me not to leave until the baby was born. But after her gall bladder surgery and as the months wore on, it became apparent that I would stay home to see her through this last birth. I wouldn't be going to college in the fall.

I didn't know it then, but my mother and I were in for a difficult year.

lou mandler

# Twenty-three
# Darkest Winter

My sister Diana had not yet left for her junior year of college on the September morning my father called up the stairs, "Girls, I'm taking Mama in to the hospital." Diana and I waited at home all day with five-year-old Susan. Ten-year-old Lillian and sixteen-year-old Betsy took the bus to school and home again. As darkness was falling, my father came back. We knew better than to expect to hear news of Mama immediately. He put his hat away. He arranged the mail on the chest freezer in the utility room. Then he said with a pleased smile, "Well, you have a baby brother."

A boy! The news was enough to stop thought.

A few days after Grant's birth, Diana left for Havre and college. Trying not to think of my classmates who were also departing our section of the Hi-Line for school or work, I settled in for what I thought would be six weeks of helping out until my mother was stronger. I had made the grudging decision that since I wasn't going to college, I would do as my sister Vivien had done. When I was free, I would go to Helena and find work.

This fall was the third period that my mother, years later, included in her list of happiest times. Certainly Mama basked in the attention that she and Daddy received for finally having a second boy; she beamed with satisfaction as she told us that Dr. Messinger had insisted on carrying Grant out to show Daddy. And she smiled with pleasure over the notes and comments from friends and neighbors.

Despite my disappointment over my thwarted college plans, the fall harvest days temporarily calmed my restlessness. Besides helping my mother, I drove the truck in the field as my father combined the wheat. Waiting for my father to empty the next load of new wheat from the combine into the truck box, I read and thought. As they had so many times before, books represented a hope of a fuller, richer future life. Around me and the truck, the strips of grain stretched out before me to meet the sky, a blue and gold wonder, and I savored again the elements of sky, earth, and the ghostly power between.

By early December, I had convinced my parents that it was time for me to leave. Mama was stronger physically and although she complained about her poor vision, she had always had poor eyesight. We made an appointment with Dr. Morgan, the optometrist. Daddy would take her there after

# This Storied Land

I was gone.

I had been in Helena a few days when a phone call came from home. Dr. Morgan, alarmed by my mother's drastic loss of vision, had sent her to a specialist who diagnosed a detached retina and ordered immediate surgery. At that time, convalescing from retina surgery meant being immobilized for a period of time, and then wearing an eye patch with a pinpoint opening in it for weeks. Mama would not be able to care for her new son, my three younger sisters, or her house. My father, mother, and younger siblings needed me at home. Subjugating my desire for a new life to my family's needs, I boarded the train for the five hundred mile trip north.

I would be home for five more months, all winter and into the spring. It was a time of muddled emotions. I played a housewife role in my mother's house at a time when I had anticipated entering and knowing the world. I disciplined my two younger sisters, Betsy and Lillian, intervening in their spats and assigning them duties—washing dishes, setting the table, picking up the front room. I played some of my mother's role towards my father, telling him when we needed carrots and potatoes from the cistern pit, what groceries we should have from town, when dinner and supper were ready. I felt too much like a mother and not enough like a daughter. I felt trapped.

Early in January we had a day of rain. Then the temperature plunged, and the standing rain turned to ice. Throughout the month of January, our yard was ice, ice which seemed to creep into the house as well.

My mother and I seemed all mixed up together that winter. She had had two surgeries and delivered a child in this, her forty-fourth year. Now, although her doctor ordered rest, her eyes were bandaged, and she was unable to read her way through the short daylight hours of these winter days. She succumbed to hopelessness. At eighteen, I had neither the experience nor the knowledge to understand my mother or to help her in her despair. I blamed her. I thought she was weak. I fought my own sense of hopelessness.

*I didn't know that Mama's eye problems made her think of her father and of the lost vision in his one eye. I learned decades later that in her fear and loneliness, she wrote him a letter expressing her understanding of his suffering. My uncle told me recently their father had said it was "the best letter I ever got."*

At the time, I poured out my feelings in a diary. Interspersed between descriptions of what I referred to as my "black and blue" moods were notes about the bits of life that kept me going—jokes my sisters had heard in school, books that Lillian brought home, my five-year-old sister's remarks on life, the pleasure I took in my baby brother's development. I painted cupboards, took my mother to doctors, washed dishes, and made meals again and again while I raged and despaired and hoped.

In her wintry helplessness, my mother made it clear that she needed me. Me who had always needed her. My world was upside down. Perhaps the inexorable departure of her children from home was also affecting my mother that winter. I, the fifth child, would tip the balance. From time to time, when she seemed better for a day or two, I broached the subject of my leaving home and was met with her frightened, "Oh, no!" The days passed, and I feared I would never live a life apart from my parents.

As happens on the prairie, one day in early March the weather provided a bit of human drama to vary our winter days. The school bus stopped at the gate as usual, but surprisingly, five, not two, children emerged. By now we could recognize my uncle Carl Olson's children, and as the group of five neared the house, we saw Marjorie, Myron, and Lloyd Olson walking with Betsy and Lillian. The bus driver had judged the dirt road to the Olsons' too slippery to attempt so he let the Olson children off at our house. My mother seemed quite pleased to see them. Clearly, whatever sins their grandmother had committed, Mama didn't see the grandchildren as guilty too. She had had one of her good days and had baked cupcakes.

"You must be hungry," she said to her brother's children as she offered the plate of after-school sweets. As they gobbled the cupcakes up, her face showed the satisfaction of the appreciated baker. Mama watched these children with obvious curiosity. When their mother Laura came to pick them up, my mother responded with friendliness.

"The children can stay here any time the road to your place is impassable," she said.

Laura voiced an invitation to visit the Olson farm, and my mother neither accepted nor refused. That her and her brother's children now rode the school bus together established a kind of communication between the families, but my mother didn't visit her girlhood home that year.

Spring came. In mid-April I helped my father plant a

lawn. I planted canna lilies and gladiola, and my father transplanted a vine honeysuckle. We had some sunny, warm days. My three sisters and I went for a walk in the pastures. Susan and I picked crocuses and ran down all the hills. On the top of Eagle Hill I extolled the beauty of the skies to Betsy. I made my sisters lie flat on their backs with me to look at the sky. Then I said, "Try looking at the world this way." I spread my legs and bent from the waist to see the upside-down world I'd created from this perspective. It was sky, sky, sky with just a little earth. A couple days later, I saw a cow licking "the shiny stuff" from its newborn calf. We picked buttercups on the side of the big hill across from the house, this time even bringing my baby brother. "Do you know," I said to my diary, "babies never cry when they're outside." I took off the storm windows.

Then we had a day of rain which turned to snow by evening. By now, I had wrested an agreement from my parents that I could leave at the end of April. Although she had capitulated to my strong-minded determination, my mother still dreaded my going, and in my last couple weeks at home she often sat with me in the kitchen as we did the daily chores. That day, when the spring rain turned to winter snow, my mother, almost as though she felt I must not leave her until I finally knew her own truth, began to tell me stories from her secret well.

She started with the first time she and Daddy met. She was just twelve; he was an overall-clad youth of nineteen. Pa and Ma Wiedeman and their five children had just moved from across the North Dakota line to Montana, just a couple miles from the Olsons. Grandma Olson, always eager to be the first to meet new folks, brought her family over to meet the Wiedemans. On the way home, my mother announced to her family, "I like the one with overalls." As my mother matured and continued to think well of this quiet, handsome young man, it was also clear that a relationship between them could not develop smoothly. The Wiedemans lived according to The Truth, and my mother's parents were staunch Lutherans.

I thought of my mother's Confirmation picture in the desk drawer. The finery she wore—shoes, stockings, dress, and corsage—must have represented a huge expense for her poor parents. Yes, being a Lutheran was important.

My parents began their courtship in the spring, when my mother was sixteen and my father was twenty-three. Mama was working as a live-in hired girl for the Hunters at the time. My father was able to visit her there away from the disfavor with which her parents regarded him. We knew my mother had always revered Mr. Hunter, and now, nearly thirty years later, she said with satisfied pride, "Mr. Hunter liked Daddy." During the next two years my mother worked for a succession of farm families—the Ottens, the Soderquists, the Lesters, the Hedges.

Grandpa and Grandma Olson's discovery that my father and his family didn't observe Christmas deepened their disapproval of the developing relationship between their daughter and the younger Wiedeman brother. Not only were the Wiedemans not Lutherans, but ignoring Christmas seemed to the Olsons to be non-Christian. When Mama and Daddy decided to marry, my mother's parents objected. My parents would have to wait for my mother to turn eighteen. She and my father set their wedding date for the day after my mother's eighteenth birthday, March 3rd, and the date was engraved on my mother's wedding ring. On that day, a spring blizzard came up, blocking the roads. They reset their wedding day for a week later.

The day before their wedding, my mother walked the couple miles from the Olson farm to Rock Spring School. The young teacher there was sympathetic to Mama and her marriage plans and had agreed to do Mama's hair for her wedding day. The teacher arranged my mother's dark hair in an orderly and stylish wave. Mama had used her hired-girl money to buy a pink crepe dress and a band of artificial flowers for her hair. Early the next morning, she walked away from her father's house, down the curving dirt driveway to the road to meet the pickup driven by my father. Daddy's sister and Mama's cousin, who would be witnesses to the marriage, were passengers in the pickup.

"My folks kept putting pressure on me not to marry him, and Daddy knew it. When he drove to our place that morning, he looked awful. His face was something because he was afraid I wasn't going to go with him. He thought I might give in to my folks," my mother said. Then she finished fiercely, "but I told him, 'I'm going with you!'"

Some drifts from the earlier storm remained on the roads. They bulldozed through them in the pickup. It took a long time to travel the thirteen miles to Plentywood. Once there, they changed their clothes, went to the courthouse, and found the judge who married them. Then they went to the City Café for a meal and drove back to the Wiedemans' farm. Upset by the marriage and upset that my parents weren't married by a preacher, Grandpa and Grandma Olson wrote a letter to Grandpa and Grandma Wiedeman that my mother said "was just awful." Grandpa and Grandma Wiedeman went to see the Olsons, but three weeks went by before the Olsons came to visit their daughter and her new husband. The familial relationship resumed.

The Hanson place, the newly married couple's first home, was within a few miles of both the Olsons and the Wiedemans. Both Mama's and Daddy's mothers were energetic women, but in very different ways. Ma Wiedeman modeled domestic order. Not so Grandma Olson. I had never heard my mother speak well of her mother. But today there was near admiration in her voice as she said of her, "Why, she would help the calves get born, work in the fields, build fence, and then take the horse and buggy to Rostad to catch up on the news. She thought nothing of taking the wagon twenty miles to Coalridge to get a load of coal. And what a memory she had. She could remember dates just like that."

Then Mama grinned a wicked grin and added, "Your uncle Hans always said you have to be smart to be that crazy."

The grin was soon replaced by a scowl, and Mama said, "But you know, everyone has their faults, and she could find them. She'd get mad at someone and she'd stand with her feet like so," my mother planted her feet a foot apart, "and her hands would be agoing and she'd just give it to them."

My two grandmothers displayed their differences in spades during the following winter. My mother, newly pregnant, was suffering her first and probably her worst-ever bout with morning sickness. Day after day she threw up what nourishment she forced down. By April, the racking spasms of vomiting had robbed her of both weight and spirit. At a hundred and five pounds, she was easy for my father to carry each day to the chair he had put in the spring sun. He propped her legs up and coaxed her to drink the beef broth he had prepared.  He brought the doctor out.

His mother came nearly every day for a time to care for her daughter-in-law and do housework.  "She wasn't sure I was going to live," my mother said.  Grandma Olson, on the other hand, stayed away and sent the Lutheran preacher out to see her daughter.  The preacher happened to arrive at a time when Ma Wiedeman was there.  He did his pastoral duty as he saw it, reciting The Lord's Prayer with my mother.  She obediently folded her hands, but anger at her mother and embarrassment that Ma Wiedeman was witnessing this Lutheran scene prevented her from vocalizing or even mouthing the words.

By May, my mother had regained her appetite.  "When I started eating, I ate like a horse," she said.  The ten-pound baby, my sister Agnes, was born in October.  Agnes's baby book records the gifts brought by relatives, including Grandma and Grandpa Olson.  And our early photo albums show pictures of Grandma and Grandpa Olson with my three oldest siblings when they were very small children.  It wasn't until six years later that the final break would come.

Mama had said enough for the day.  But this was just the beginning of what she told me from her secret story well.

# This Storied Land

lou mandler

# Twenty-four
# Drawing Deep from the Story Well

A few mornings after she told the story of her marriage, my mother had a particularly blue day. We were in the kitchen again. I was washing dishes. Her thoughts, when she spoke, were of old troubles, old hurts, of feeling helpless to assuage or prevent these old wrongs.

My memory begins with her comment, "You know Daddy went through a rebellious period when he was young. He left home for awhile when he wasn't very old."

"I knew something had happened," she said. "Your aunt Edna told me that a visitor to the Wiedemans' used to pick on Daddy." Edna was the wife of my father's brother.

"This man would tease Daddy and torment him, and Daddy was so sensitive that it really bothered him."

My mother felt there was more than just taunts between this man and Daddy.

"I asked Aunt Tillie and she never told me, and I asked Olga Peterson and she didn't say much, but she did say, 'I told Mrs. Wiedeman that she'd better watch out or the same thing would happen to Fredricka." Fredricka was my father's younger sister.

"What would happen to Fredricka?" I asked.

"Well, no one ever really told me, but I think I know," my mother said. "Daddy used to go out and walk in the pastures whenever he came, and Daddy could hardly bear to hear his name."

"I think I know why," she said again, and her lips clamped shut in the way they did when she was thinking about something shameful.

I had finished the dishes by now and the task no longer kept me a prisoner in the kitchen to hear my mother's sad stories. I fled upstairs to mull this over. This was the way my mother acted when something involved with sex came up, but what could it be?

I couldn't figure this puzzle out when I was eighteen.


*Toward the end of her life, my mother told me the same story, through the same pursed lips and with the same knowing, pained look in her eye. Again she spoke of the visitor to the Wiedeman home when Daddy was a child, a man who was influential and respected by others, but whose name brought an abrupt change in my father's demeanor and whose presence Daddy avoided. Again she said with conviction, "And I'm sure I know what happened." About such things, however, Mama veered towards silence, not story. In the silence that followed, I suddenly understood that Mama had pieced together bits of old conversations, her own observations, and her knowledge of her husband to draw the conclusion that when Daddy was young, he had been sexually molested by this family friend.*

*Her conviction helped explain her fiercely protective attitude towards her independent husband and the decisiveness with which she and Daddy had confronted Bruce's molestation of the little girls at Hunter school years before. And perhaps it helped explain why my father seemed to harbor an undercurrent of sadness and pain.*

In our next session of kitchen chores, I strove to avert any more tales of regret or of wounds that hadn't healed. I wanted good stories. I primed the pump by asking about the families Mama had mentioned working for. In the winding way of stories, she soon stumbled into talk of Rostad, the little town north and west of Hunter.

"Rostad was a rough place," Mama said. "Hunter wasn't like that. It had a better class of people. Rostad had the Stewarts. Old Mrs. Stewart was something else again. People said all kinds of things about her. They found a human skeleton on the land there, and people said she had something to do with it."

Then she launched into her memories of another Rostad resident. "Emma LeBrun's husband, Louie Dalby, went to the state pen in Deer Lodge for shooting a cowboy in a bar in Rostad. Then when he got out, they rented the Hanson place from Daddy for five dollars a month. Mr. Halskov was sick at the time and he hired Daddy to run his threshing crew. Louie Dalby came looking for a job, and Daddy hired him. Then when it came time to settle up, Louie said, 'Well, I s'pose you want your rent money now.' Daddy said he did and Louie said, 'Well, I had a lot of cleaning up to do after that skunk got in.' So I don't know if Daddy ever got his five dollars."

Her thoughts drifted closer to home, "A lot of those cowboys and Wobblies (members of the Industrial Workers of the World who worked in the agricultural West) and outlaws would stop at the folks'. Some of the Wobblies in the '20s were good and some weren't. One of them got into the house when my folks were gone and took my mother's engagement ring to sell it. Well, one of the others came and got my folks and said, 'You better come down here.'

"Frank Coleman, a cousin of Jesse James, stayed with the folks for a while. He had worked on a threshing crew and had gotten to know the folks. When he lived with us, he would take a team of horses down to Coalridge, stay with the miners, and haul coal up to Hunter to sell."

And then her story line roped in the Morgans. "Some of the cowboys stopped at my folks' because it was on the way to the Morgans', which was a real gathering place and all kinds of things went on there. Mrs. Joe wouldn't put up with a lot of it, some of those other people who hung out there! For instance, Tom Mudd was a nice-appearing man and easy to get along with but. . ." Mama was silent.

I waited, and sure enough, she went on, "People think he killed a man. The wagon-box murder, they called it.

A young man from the east was shot while driving into town. People think he was going in to the sheriff to talk about what was going on out there." Again she was silent for a moment.

"Then when his son ran for sheriff—well, it's a good thing he didn't get it."

And after another pause, "But Joe Morgan. He might have had his faults, but he was sure good to us."

I knew that Joe Morgan had come to our farm a few times to help when a cow was having trouble calving or when a heifer was sick with bloat, but there seemed to be more behind my mother's comment.

"What do you mean?" I asked.

"Well, in the trouble with my folks, it was Joe Morgan who helped Daddy."

"How? What did he do?"

With her heart and mind already in her story, Mama kept talking, starting at the beginning, telling what we had wondered about for years.

"You know my mother never liked Daddy. But she probably knew he didn't like her. And she didn't like me because I stood up to her. Grandpa Lindvall—of course he was her father—didn't like me either. But my dad did. And Grandma Lindvall did; I went up there every day after her stroke and helped her out. Grandma Lindvall used to talk to me about all kinds of things. She remembered that when she was still in the old country the Laplanders used to ski down to where her family lived in Sweden, looking for food."

Then Mama veered back to thoughts of her parents. "Well, even after all that nonsense when we were married and just the way she was, we still went to see my folks, and Daddy helped them out some, fixing the machinery and this and that.

But my mother, she had a way of making trouble."

She went on to tell about February of 1942, twenty years earlier, when my sister Diana was born.  Five days after Diana's birth, my mother's sister Emily gave birth to her first child, our cousin Rachel.. None of us Wiedeman children were baptized as infants.  It wasn't the way of The Truth, and although my parents hadn't professed at that time, my mother no longer followed the way of the Lutheran faith in which she had been baptized and confirmed.  That their grandchildren were not baptized upset my Olson grandparents, and when Rachel was born, Grandpa and Grandma Olson certainly expected that this grandchild would be baptized Lutheran.

Soon after Rachel's birth, my father and Emily's husband Hans went together to the Olson farm to pick up a piece of machinery and a cow that the Olsons had wintered for Hans and Emily.  There were five in the yard that day.  Besides my father and Hans, both my grandparents and my Uncle Carl stood together talking.  Grandma Olson, on her way to the barnyard to do chores, was carrying a heavy metal pail.  In the course of visiting about Rachel's birth, she asked Hans when the baptism would be.  Hans and Emily had decided between themselves that there would be no baptism.  Upon hearing this, Grandma Olson was beside herself.  Thinking, quite wrongly my mother said, that my father had influenced this decision, she turned to him and exploded with rage.

"She could really be hateful," my mother said.  "And she really talked rough sometimes, too.  Well, I guess she called him every ugly, vicious name she could think of."

When Daddy's mother-in-law had exhausted her considerable powers of speech, she flung the metal pail she was carrying at my father's head. It hit him in the temple, and blood flowed.

"And then of course he had to defend himself," my mother said.

My father slapped my grandmother across her face. Hard.

I was stunned. I couldn't believe my father would do such a thing. My father never hit anyone.

Alarmed by my father's response, Grandma Olson's husband and son leapt to her defense while Hans stood by my father. No other physical injuries occurred, but the damage had been done.

My mother continued her story. "Then my folks went to town to the sheriff's office and wrote out a complaint and the sheriff came out and arrested Daddy for assault. It was just awful. And it was really hard on Daddy. You know how he is."

The pain and humiliation of that long-ago day contorted her face.

It was Joe Morgan who went into town and bailed Daddy out of jail.

My mind tried to reconcile this new picture of my father in jail with the mild but heroic picture of him which had been etched in my mind all my life.

After a reflective pause, Mama finished her story. "And then she went all over the country talking about how mean her kids were to her."

So this was the drama that ushered in the years of silence. I thought of the characters involved; my wild Swedish grandmother, her obedient husband, my proud father, and, waiting at home, Daddy's fiercely loyal wife, who had felt spurned and embarrassed by her mother all her life. My mother, who so wanted to soothe Daddy's earlier wounds, had not been able to protect him from her own mother.

Mama had one last surprise for me. Perhaps the thought that she might never see her loved father again after their move to Kalispell made her "do the right thing." She told me that after her parents moved, "I wrote to them and told them I forgave them."

I didn't ask and she didn't say whether they replied.


*Nearly forty years later, after Mama's death, I found a couple of letters from her father tucked in amongst the things in her dresser drawer. One was written shortly before he became incapacitated by a stroke when he was in his eighties. Grandma Olson outlived her husband by several years.*

# This Storied Land

lou mandler

## Twenty-five
## Scent of Sage

*. . . We can ask and ask but we can't have again what once seemed ours forever—the way things looked. . . a remembered voice, the touch of a hand, a loved face. They've gone and you can only wait for the pain to pass. . . So, in memory, it stays as I left it.*

—J. L. Carr, *A Month in the Country*

On the one hand, April 23rd, the day I would leave my childhood home behind, stood in my imagination as a tall gate, open and beckoning to the rich experiences on the other side. On the other hand, I fretted to my diary that I might be leaving to work in Helena before Mama was able to care for the two little ones. I gave my sixteen-year-old sister a pep talk about how important it would be to do the dishes at night and to help care for Susan and Grant.

I wavered between wanting to enter the world and wondering whether my timing was too cruel. I had consulted my siblings; some thought I should leave, and others thought I was being too hasty. Spring's coming stirred feelings of urgency. If I stayed, I feared the months would turn to years, and my mother would never feel that it was time for me to go. I felt like I was running for my life.

These days when I pack to go back East after a visit home, I often tuck a bit of sage into my suitcase for its long-lasting, pungent scent. Then I packed my graduation suitcases with just my small wardrobe and the Bible which my Grandmother Wiedeman had given me for my high school graduation nearly a year earlier. On the flyleaf, she had written, "My Dear Grand-daughter. I hope you will like this bible. I could think of nothing more useful to give you. There is one little verse in the 3rd Epistle of John, verse 4, that expresses what brings joy to me too as well as it did, to the writer of this epistle." (*I have no greater joy than to hear that my children walk in truth.*) I still have the Bible. I no longer walk in The Truth.

My mother sprinkled my last days at home with comments which were alternately acerbic and emotional. As I sorted through my clothes, I cast aside a black and rust patterned cotton dress, and my mother observed, "You sure did a lot of work in that dress."

# This Storied Land

As she eyed my eagerness to go forth, she commented, "Life is just as real in this country as it is in any city, you know."

On the day before my departure, my mother was feeling very blue and burst out with, "I hope you don't get a job so you'll have to come home!"

During my last day at home, I walked alone up Eagle Hill where I had walked so many times with my brother and sisters. I stood high in the circle of land that stretched out from my feet. My old friend the wind brushed against me. Its force spoke of life in other places. It calmed my worries. I stood for long minutes, on top of the world, with the wind in my hair, ears, clothes, bones.

It was afternoon on the late April day when my father brought me with my suitcases into Plentywood to catch the "Galloping Goose," the bus to the train in Culbertson. I noted in my diary that Daddy hadn't shaved. This was unusual. Because of his unshaven state, he was shy about bringing my suitcases into the depot. My mother, I wrote, had cried only a little when we said goodbye.

Three talkative women sat behind me on the bus to Culbertson, but I paid them no heed. I was thinking about the road I was traveling. I felt the wrench of the freshly pulled root, but I was thinking I was free, free of household chores, of a constricted life. I didn't know then that I had brought more with me than what I had chosen to put in my Sears Roebuck suitcases. I didn't realize that entering the world would be like a walk home from Eagle Hill. Sometimes we plucked wild flowers—bluebells, crocuses, grandpa's whiskers—and brought them home, but we couldn't help bringing back the scent of sage and the feel of the wind, the burrs and prairie

# lou mandler

needles sticking to our socks. The plucked wild flowers are a choice. The feel of the wind, the scent of sage, the burrs and prairie needles are not. I didn't know then that the pictures and silences and stories—my stories, my mother's stories—were coming with me.

# Epilogue
## The Life Force

Mama and winter sparred until the end of her life. In her late seventies, she flew to San Diego at the beginning of winter for lung surgery. For months she had been breathing with the aid of oxygen, but she hadn't lost her style of grit with a twist. As she left home, her parting words to our father were, "Well, I'll be back. Dead or alive!" She came back alive, physically weaker but with her spirit intact. That winter was extraordinarily snowy. Storm after storm came in until the snow nearly covered the bay window in the living room. My father had to shovel his way out of the house through the snowbank covering the front door.

During one of these storms, when travel was impossible, my mother wasn't feeling well. Always sensible and never afraid to face reality with a wry comment, she said to my sister Susan, "If I die during this storm, just close my bedroom door and keep the room cold."

A little over a year later, she became ill in the middle of a raging blizzard. Unable to sleep or rest, she talked, and her words became a torrent; she spoke incessantly about the neighbors, the Morgans, her kids, her work. Wind-driven snow drifted against the house and made the roads impassable. Agnes, Susan, and my father spent two sleepless nights caring for her. When the weather cleared, the ambulance followed the snowplow out to the farm. Mama walked through the snow to the ambulance which took her in to the hospital.

Within weeks, she was in the nursing home. When I first visited my mother there, she had lost the fluidity of her speech and thought, but she was still Mama in what she said and how she said it. She worried aloud about the welfare of her children. She talked about wanting to be home with Daddy. She spoke of a family dog of years ago—Peppy, "a good dog for kids." She talked about work. She said, "You know Daddy says that Gus Rosgard is a slowpoke. That he never gets anything done. He doesn't keep his fences up." She went on to plead, "I want to go home," and returned to the topic of work. "You were a worker," she said to me. Then, "Is Daddy here? He said Chris Tufton was a good worker. He says Chris sure beats Gus Rosgard." And then a spirited, "I'm a stubborn Swede."

One morning that summer when I arrived at the nursing home, one of the aides said, "Your mother was calling for Philip last night." They were to be apart for only a few more weeks.   At the end of the summer, my father had another stroke and he, too, entered the home.

Other residents of the nursing home had familiar names and faces.  Garnet King told me from her wheelchair that she and my mother used to ride horses together when they were girls.  "Your mother was quite a rider," she said. Garnet's husband Howard drove our school bus for many years.  He chewed snuff, and once we were out the bus door, he often sent a stream of brown tobacco after us into the dirt. In the nursing home, his spit cup was attached to his wheelchair.  "Was I all right?" he asked me.  "I tried to watch my language around you girls."

I knew the names of some of the other residents, not from my own knowledge but because I'd heard them in my mother's stories—the Juves, the Lutnesses.  Newton and Nova Doyle's daughter Mary was there.  My uncle Carl's mother-in-law, Laura Olson's mother.  Raymond Houth, friendly and upbeat at ninety, visited the nursing home occasionally.   So did my fourth grade teacher who remembered my beating the boys in races at school.  One of the nurses who helped care for my mother in her last, tortured days was Joe Morgan's granddaughter.

The day before my mother died, my sister Agnes brought out a note that Mama had written while she was in the Billings hospital three years earlier, awaiting preliminary lung surgery. Written on three small 3x5-inch pages torn from one of the spiral notebooks she used so often, it was just a few sentences:"August 2nd, 12:30 nite," it said, "I've been thinking, as long as I can kind of be able to take care of myself, come to table, go to bathroom, can talk, not lose my mind. . . help me to live. If I can be a help to people, there are some I know I can help and give encouragement to. But if I am in a condition I am a burden, don't help me to live. I don't fear death and no one should grieve when I go. Daddy, you have helped me to a better life, both spiritually and to have the children who all have been a precious gift. Sometimes it's been hard but we need that to appreciate God's help that he can give us."

On the morning of the last day of my mother's life, I awoke at four and waited for the dawn. When the land began receiving the light of the sun, I walked north to Eagle Hill. There was a good wind. Once on top of Eagle Hill, I could see nearly the entire section of country where my mother had lived her life. Plentywood wasn't quite visible but just a few miles to the south I could see the hills surrounding the coulee where Grandpa and Grandma Olson had spent forty years of their lives and where my mother was born. Less than a mile to the west was the farm where my mother had worked for W.D. Hunter. A mile north I could see the Hunter Cemetery where Mr. Hunter was buried and where, in a few days, just a few feet from him, my mother would lie forever. In the middle was the land on which my parents had lived and loved and worked and raised us. I thought of my two strong grandmothers, whose characters and actions had stamped their influence not only on their children but on their children's children, of my two mild-mannered grandfathers, whose gentleness lived on in the generations they begot.

I wondered how long the sky and wind and earth would accommodate its human guests. How long till only the stories remain? Or would the stories too be taken by time and the wind?

The rock formations the Indians had made so long ago still faintly marked the brow of the hill. Set among them was a cement marker placed by the U.S. Geological Survey. I stood in the midst of these monuments, in the dawn of a new day, knowing Mama would not be alive tomorrow, wondering how that could be, that the world would not hold her.

My mother died at the beginning of winter, on her father's birthday. It didn't seem fair that, after a lifetime battling sickness, her dying should require a struggle of several days. But some spirits are hard to extinguish. The first snow of the season fell on the day of her funeral. As the earth-colored hearse carrying our mother's body led the caravan of cars curving past Mama's and Daddy's farm and north to the Hunter graveyard, the world was dusted with white. The fields and garden were fallow.

Before Mama's final illness, when Daddy was eighty-four, his second stroke hit him while he was working in the shop. One leg was partially paralyzed so he crawled the thirty yards down to the house, and Mama called the ambulance. He was hospitalized for a few days. The day he returned home, the paralysis gone, he went out to the field to summerfallow.

He was nearly eighty-eight when he joined Mama in the nursing home. He could walk and feed himself. He could speak some. He was almost totally deaf. But he wiped tears from Susan's face and put his arm around me as we three stood beside Mama in the moments after she died.

When I visited Montana the summer after Mama died, my father was nearly ninety. Susan had told me that she is haunted by the memory of Mama saying to her once in the nursing home, "Will I never see home again?" We decided that we would bring my father out to the farm as often as we could during my visit.

The first time we took him home, where my sisters now lived, Susan drove the fifteen miles slowly. My father was alert, looking at farm machinery and the crops in the fields, checking our route. Once home, he headed for the top of the hill behind the house. The grass was high. His former strength was diminished, and we followed, wondering if we could manage if he fell. He walked through the tall grass, stopping occasionally to check the garden, the trees he had planted behind the house, the shop, the tractor standing idle in the yard. He looked at it all and gazed over the land to the horizon. He was steady on his feet.

I keep my photographs in an old trunk, not a desk drawer. Like my mother, I haven't taken the time to frame or display the important ones; I can see them without looking at them. One is of my parents on the open prairie during their courtship. My mother wears a flowered dress, my father a white shirt with open collar. He is standing behind her, his hands clasped around her waist. The wind blows their hair. They look proud to be together. Another photo is of my parents in their old age. It is taken from behind. My father is wearing blue overalls and a blue chambray work shirt, my mother a pastel dress. They are watching the harvesting of the grain in the field before them. If one looks closely, my mother's oxygen line is visible. They sit side by side.

# This Storied Land

lou mandler

# About the Author...

Lou Mandler was born and raised in Montana. A graduate of Montana State University, she has also lived in Colorado, Alberta, and Idaho. Graduate study at Middlebury College's Bread Loaf School of English initiated a move to Connecticut where she has lived since. She has been a secretary, an English teacher, and is currently an educational administrator at Canterbury School. She has received a Joseph Klingenstein Fellowship to Teacher's College of Columbia University, a Geraldine R. Dodge Fellowship for Secondary School Teachers, and a grant to a National Endowment for the Humanities Seminar.

Printed in the United States
19626LVS00002B/313-318